THE
SAMURAI
LEADER

WINNING BUSINESS
BATTLES WITH THE
WISDOM,
HONOR
AND COURAGE
OF THE SAMURAI CODE

BILL DIFFENDERFFER

SOURCEBOOKS, INC.®
NAPERVILLE, ILLINOIS

Published by Sourcebooks, Inc.
P.O. Box 4410, Naperville, Illinois 60567-4410
(630) 961-3900
FAX: (630) 961-2168
www.sourcebooks.com

Library of Congress Cataloging-in-Publication Data
Diffenderffer, Bill.
  Winning business battles with the wisdom, honor, and courage of the samurai code / Bill Diffenderffer.
     p. cm.
  Includes bibliographical references.
  ISBN-13: 978-1-4022-0546-0
  ISBN-10: 1-4022-0546-5
  1. Business ethics. 2. Leadership—Moral and ethical aspects. 3. Management—Moral and ethical aspects. 4. Success in business. 5. Samurai—Conduct of life. I. Title.

HF5387.D5445 2005
174'.4—dc22

                                        2005025119

Printed and bound in the United States of America
LB 10 9 8 7 6 5 4 3 2 1

This book is dedicated to my mother, who taught me to love books, and to my father, who showed me what it is to be samurai...and to Alicia, Ann, Bonnie, Caren, Mary Jo, and Terra, my companions on the journey.

CONTENTS

INTRODUCTION

Translations and adaptations of works by Sun Tzu, Machiavelli, Confucius, and Napoleon, to name just a few, have provided valuable insights and strategies relevant to meeting the challenges of corporate life. Similarly, the lives and the teachings of the samurai warriors from the twelfth century through the end of the eighteenth century offer a unique and powerful model from which the managers of today's business have much to learn. In particular, the Code of the Samurai provides a foundation for a way of being that will lead managers to achieving greater levels of success than they had previously imagined themselves capable.

It has never been tougher to be a good manager than it is now. Technological revolution, global competition, new business models, stricter standards for raising capital, tighter labor markets, increasing competition for fewer and fewer leadership positions—all have raised the bar for what it takes to succeed in business today. Add to that the post Enron-WorldCom-Martha Stewart environment, with its heightened necessity for legal and moral compliance to vague standards of behavior, and the challenge of management becomes truly daunting.

Given the challenges confronting managers today, there is a need for performance models that can provide guidelines for behavior. These models can be real or fictional or mythologized blends of the two. Earlier generations of managers had the Horatio Alger stories, preaching that hard work and virtuous actions would lead to business success. Then came the almost mythic careers of Henry Ford, Thomas Edison, John D. Rockefeller, Walt Disney, and a pantheon of other great businessmen whose names are carried forward in the names of current giant corporations. Even recent generations had admirable leaders like Sam Walton and the combination of William Hewlett and David Packard.

But today the role models in business have become more ambiguous, ethically challenged, and difficult to emulate—even if worthy of emulation. Of course, there have been many terrific and honorable business leaders lately, yet too little is known of them and too much is known of the dark-sided media creations like Gordon Gekko of the movie *Wall Street* and the cast of villains associated with Enron, WorldCom, Tyco International, Adelphia Communications, and a host of other victimized companies.

Even unblemished, media identifiable, successful leaders like Jack Welch, Warren Buffet, and Lou Gerstner, while demonstrating that brilliant managers can transform huge companies (and whose stories can be found on the bookshelves), offer little as guidelines for daily behavior. They provide success stories without providing models for success.

To strive for success in business with no model or behavioral guidelines and principles in mind is to wander through a swamp with no compass. Managing through the business equivalents of quicksand, poisonous snakes, and malaria-bearing insects requires a navigational system that is structured, disciplined, complete, and dynamic.

Where can managers find such a career-long navigating guide? Perhaps, realistically, they are on their own; the business world now too diverse, too complex, too exacting for any role model to be useful. Do your best and good luck! Somebody has to win. Maybe it will be you—or at least some derivative of you ten years from now after you've experienced a lifetime of stress and frustration, conflicted personal priorities, and compromised ethics and values. (OUCH! That even hurts to write!)

Sometimes the best answer to a problem is one that has worked well in the past. Few challenges facing humankind have no precedent—particularly when it comes to struggling for survival and success. Nothing about competition is new. Updating lessons from history has the advantage of offering battle-hardened, time-tested solutions. When history offers a lesson that is on point, it is wise to learn it.

The Concept of a Code

The Samurai Code was both formal and informal. It developed organically and was mostly communicated by word of mouth, by way of stories of true

"samurai" deeds. It was treated with the utmost seri-
ousness. The principles by which samurai were to
guide their actions were clear, comprehensive, and
rather rigid. The penalty for a samurai who did not
conform to the code could be very severe. In
sixteenth-century Japan, it could get one killed.
Interestingly, there is no such thing as a leader code
for doing business, not even an unofficial one. Yet,
codes are not unfamiliar to us. There was the Code
of the West. The Boy Scouts have a code, Girl Scouts
too. Most militaries have both formal and informal
codes. Doctors have the Hippocratic oath and even
lawyers have one. However, nothing for managers
has evolved, and that's a problem.

It's a problem because most managers really need
one. It is very hard to be a good manager in today's
business environment. There are so many and varied
actions to be taken, judgments to be made, and situations to be handled. How can one make all the right
decisions? How can one be consistent and fair? These
are very important attributes in a manager.

There are those who believe that everything is sit-
uational. What works best depends on the circumstances. Morality is relative. That kind of thinking
worked well at Enron and WorldCom—for a while.
Then everything crashed and burned. The problem is
that most managers are better than that, but it's easy
to get lost when there are no consistent standards, no
measuring guideposts, no code of behavior.

So why isn't there a code for managers? And if there were a code, would it make a difference? **Will having a code make you a better manager?**

The reason there is no code for managers is simple. Most business people believe that adhering to a code would limit their ability to get what they want—which in most cases means limiting their ability to make money. The funny thing is that for most people, that belief is not true.

"Let me get this right. You're saying managers don't have a code and they need one. Samurai had a code, but since they're not around anymore, managers should take on the Samurai Code."

That's right. But there's more to it than that. It's not an easy code to live by, let alone to manage by—since it held its followers to very high standards. And obviously, it wasn't really designed for the twenty-first-century manager. So, a few things may have to be changed. It will take some work and some instruction to get to a point where a manager realistically can act in accordance with it. But, *surprise! surprise!* **It can be done! The rewards—both monetary and personal—will be worth it!**

But there's a catch. At first, the benefits of following the Samurai Code are counter-intuitive. The message and the lessons seem much too simple to be relevant in the highly complex business environment today's managers live in. It is in this simplicity that its Zen underpinnings are most obvious. But, don't casually disregard twenty-five hundred years of intellectual development. It is a holistic system built on mutually supportive root elements. Each element taken alone is simple, but the whole is powerful and can conquer the complex. The Samurai Code was designed for warriors and it fosters the mindfulness and fearlessness a warrior needs to succeed in battles. There is nothing simple about a system that accomplishes that!

AUTHOR'S NOTE

This book contains a number of Samurai Leader stories. They are all true. They come out of *Fortune* 500 companies such as Federal Express, IBM, Continental Airlines, and Holiday Inn, as well as medium-sized companies. Several relate to events in the travel industry because of my twenty-five years of work there. Some specifically relate to SystemOne Corporation (a global provider of computer reservation and travel management systems) where I worked for twelve years, including six years as CEO.

During most of that time, SystemOne was a major subsidiary of Continental Airlines, employing several thousand people. When I first started as CEO of SystemOne, it was in chapter 11 and had just been valued in a formal bankruptcy court proceeding at $50–60 million. It had major financial problems and experts did not believe it could survive because it faced much larger competitors. Its turnaround under my leadership was dramatic. Following a series of transactions which I orchestrated, Continental received over $600 million for it. The SystemOne stories are included to provide a sense of continuity for the reader.

Additionally, the challenges SystemOne faced are representative of those confronting many middle-sized

companies. Although the *Fortune* 500 company stories relate to work at the global scale, most of the
business of America is done by small to midsize companies. Even more than the global companies, they
need to be samurai.

I also served on the senior management policy
committee of Continental as a senior vice president of
the airline and was there to observe its amazing turnaround. Again, I saw how samurai behavior drove
success, even when the odds were strongly against it.
Later I was a vice president at IBM, one of the leaders of its business consulting group, and was there for
the last stage of its remarkable story under Lou
Gerstner.

During my twenty-five years in business, I've
worked with over twenty CEOs of *Fortune* 500 companies and hundreds of their senior executives. I've
seen dazzling successes and dismaying failures. In so
many of the success stories, the leader's samurai characteristics stand out. In contrast and equally evident
was that in so many of the failures the roots glaringly
lie in non-samurai actions: leaders that backed away
from necessary battles, executives who didn't care
about their employees, brilliant minds that demonstrated no wisdom, selfish egos loyal to no one, and
combative personalities with no self-control or moral
principles.

CHAPTER ONE

SAMURAI AND LEADERSHIP

A SAMURAI LEADER? IS THIS FOR REAL?

Just as any business goal needs an "end" vision, so too do managers need a vision of what they want to become. It is not enough to just want to become vice president of sales or CEO. Who are you when you get there? Managers need to hold in their minds a leadership model to which they adhere during the challenging times. This book will show how the characteristics of a samurai can make you a powerful leader. It will show how acting "samurai" can directly promote success in a business environment. It will show how a manager can become a samurai in today's business world, vanquish the competition, and rise all the way to CEO if that's what that manager wants.

The Samurai Image

The image of a samurai as the ultimate warrior is well known. But samurai were also lords of vast estates (think CEOs), military commanders (think VPs of sales), administrators (middle and upper managers), and patrons of the arts and sciences. Samurai ran Japan from about the twelfth century AD through the middle of the nineteenth century—a time that included centuries-long periods of continuous warfare and centuries-long periods of peace. As a member of a warrior class, bravery in battle and skill in the martial arts were important, but equally so were honor, loyalty, honesty, integrity, and compassion. In fact, Bushido—the code of the samurai— included, in addition to those just mentioned, a rigid adherence to values such as politeness, selflessness, and respect for family and institutions. As a codified set of values for the modern corporate manager, it has few rivals.

The ideal of the samurai is not exclusive to Japan. It certainly had its counterpart in China, and the medieval knight of Europe shared many characteristics. The paradigm was even more closely matched by the classic American cowboy and the Code of the West. What could be more samurai-like than Gary Cooper in the movie *High Noon*? At the risk of death, his rigid sense of duty compelled him to fight against what appeared to be insurmountable odds. His self-respect left him no other choice.

In fact, Hollywood has long understood the similarity of the cowboy and the samurai. *The Magnificent Seven,* certainly one of the best westerns of all time, is an almost identical remake of Akira Kurosawa's classic *Seven Samurai.* Clint Eastwood is another who shared the samurai character. The first of his movie westerns, *A Fistful of Dollars,* was a remake of *Yojimbo,* another of Kurosawa's samurai movies—but in this case, the samurai was a *ronin,* a samurai without an employer that tended to be more rogue and independent.

Samurai Leaders

But what does this have to do with becoming a better manager? Everything! As the ancient Greek philosopher Heraclitus said, "A man's character is his fate." Moreover, the fundamental characteristics of a good leader/manager have not changed in thousands of years. Julius Caesar could run General Electric. Tokugawa Ieyasu would make a great CEO of IBM. Sun Tzu would know how to mount a hostile corporate takeover. Abraham Lincoln could manage through a corporate turnaround.

Industry experience and expertise is important, of course, but it is not enough. Character counts. Courage and the respect of others matter. Acting honorably can be a differentiator—and leads to a better way of living one's life. Samurai understood the importance of individual character at an institutional level better than anyone—and were very successful for five hundred years as a result.

Samurai lived and worked in a highly structured organizational unit—a clan. Identification with the clan was based on family ties, geographical boundaries, and hiring on as retainers. Each clan competed with other clans for power and wealth. For many, winning and losing was a matter of survival. The whole clan was at risk. If bad decisions were made, if alliances turned out to be unreliable, if battles were lost, the fate of the clan could be disastrous. In that environment, the behavior of the samurai became a critical success factor. The Code of the Samurai was developed over long combative centuries to promote behavior optimum for both the individual samurai and for the organization the samurai served (the clan's needs and power structure ensured that). The same needs and issues exist today for managers trying to succeed in the highly competitive environment of modern corporations.

The characteristics that made someone a very good samurai in the seventeenth century are the same characteristics that will make someone a very good manager in the twenty-first century. Though at first that may seem somewhat of a stretch, you'll discover here that sometimes an idea comes in a strange package from an unlikely source that can empower individuals to reach their highest level of potential. Just as the brilliance of ancient Greece was buried in the rubble and almost forgotten for long centuries until it was once more rediscovered, so too were powerful lessons from the samurai forgotten over time. But those lessons uniquely enable individuals to rise above trivial fears and to see through murky and cluttered circumstances. Those lessons facilitate coming up with the right solutions and then acting on them. For managers, it's the secret pathway through the mountains that separates them from their goals. (But the secret is written in code!)

What You Will Learn

This book will help an ordinary person become a samurai—and then a samurai leader!

Here's what you will learn as you journey through this book:

- The characteristics of a samurai (and how they are acquired) will be fully explained
- The relevance of these characteristics (e.g., bravery, honesty, compassion) to management will be demonstrated—and practical business advice will link the characteristics to optimal management behaviors
- The way to becoming samurai will be offered (the code will get cracked!)

Throughout the book, you will come across Samurai Stories, Samurai Leader Stories, and Sword Strokes. The Samurai Stories date back to the sixteenth and seventeenth centuries and tell of occurrences relating to real samurai whose actions demonstrate the Code of the Samurai. Often, these stories are immediately followed by Samurai Leader Stories, which tell of true modern day business successes driven by business leaders whose actions were samurai (and reflect the same characteristics of the samurai stories), even though the business leaders profiled weren't consciously acting samurai. The stories are followed by Sword Strokes, which break down samurai behavior to provide very specific and concrete business career advice.

The overall design of the book is not only to describe the Code of the Samurai and to show its relevance to today's business environment, but also to facilitate "being samurai" so as to enable future individual success. In particular, a pathway to achieving fearlessness and mindfulness will be presented. Fearlessness is necessary because without it comes stress. Stress inhibits clarity of thought. As individuals become less fearful, their minds become unblocked, and creativity is unleashed. Mindfulness leads to improved thinking. To be "mindful" is to understand things clearly, objectively, and to comprehend things fully. Samurai were trained to achieve fearlessness and mindfulness. You will see how the

Samurai Code, taken as a whole, works at achieving the particular objectives of fearlessness and mindfulness.

This book is a leader's guide to the Samurai Code, translated to be relevant in the twenty-first century. The way of the samurai offers you not just a value system, but also a way of being that will energize, embolden, and free you to do your best work—*really!*

A SAMURAI STORY

One of Lord Matsudaira's samurai went to Kyoto on a matter of debt collection. One day while standing out front of his lodgings watching the people go by, he heard a passer-by say "Lord Matsudaira's men are involved in a fight right now!" Hearing this concerned him greatly and he asked the passer-by of the location of the fight and then hurried there. When he arrived at the scene of the fight, his companions had already been cut down and their adversaries were at the point of delivering defeat. The samurai quickly let out a yell, cut the two men down, and returned to his lodgings.

The matter was made known to an official of the shogunate (the government) who called the samurai up before him and questioned, "You gave assistance in your companion's fight and thus disregarded the government's ordinance against fighting. You abetted a fight and committed bloodshed. You broke the law. This is true beyond a doubt, isn't it?"

The samurai replied, "Although you say that I have disregarded the government's ordinance, I have by no means done so. The reason for this is that all living things value their lives, and this goes without saying for human beings. I, especially, value my life. However, I thought that to hear a rumor that one's friends are involved in a fight and to pretend not to hear this is not to preserve the Way of the Samurai, so I ran to the place of action. To shamelessly return home after seeing my friends struck down would surely have lengthened my life, but this would be disregarding the Way. In preserving the Way, one will throw away his own precious life. Thus, in order to preserve the Way and not to disregard the ordinance against samurai fighting, I quickly threw away my life at that place. I beg you to execute me immediately!"

The official was very impressed and later dismissed the matter, communicating to Lord Matsudaira, "You have a very able samurai in your service. Please treasure him." [1]

At first, this may seem a strange story to highlight. A samurai breaks the law in order to avenge his comrades who had just been defeated and were about to be beheaded. He did this knowing that he would be executed for doing so. He could have just ignored the situation. No one even would have known. Yet, it was not possible for him to ignore it. To ignore the situation would have been a violation of his belief structure. Only by acting consistent with his beliefs could he maintain his self-respect and, ultimately, the respect of others.

This story is directly applicable to managers. Managers that fail to do what they know to be "right" will lose their self-respect and the respect of others. Future chapters have much more on this.

Why Be a Samurai?

"Ok, this is all very interesting, but what problem is this book trying to solve?"

Good question. Good leaders are made, not born. Leaders learn how to lead at schools, by participating in sports, by observing other leaders, in management training programs, and generally through their experiences on the job, often by trial and error. Sometimes they even learn by reading self-help management books. The learning tends to be haphazard and random and never exhaustive—though it can be exhausting. There is so much to learn. It takes a lot to be a good leader. That's why there are so few of them.

And that's the point; there really aren't very many good managers. Go into any company and ask the rank and file, ask the middle managers, ask the senior managers: how many managers do they know who they truly respect and admire? It's always a very short list. Why is that? It's rarely due to lack of intelligence. Many bad managers are very smart. Experience is important but a lot of bad managers have a great deal of experience. A good character is very important, but everyone knows some terrific people who would be horrible to work for. The problem is that it takes a lot of different traits and abilities to be a good manager— let alone an excellent one!

Consider some of the basic personal characteristics it takes, without prioritizing, to be a good manager:

- intelligence
- leadership
- respect for others
- courage
- compassion
- honesty
- integrity
- respect of others
- loyalty
- fairness
- self discipline

That's quite a list already and it could easily be added to. But it is just a list. There is no assumption that the qualities listed are interconnected or mutually supportive. The interesting thing to note though is that it is a pretty good match to the behavior required of a samurai acting in accordance with the Samurai Code. But the Samurai Code is integrated and holistic. To borrow language from the world of high-tech software, it is robust, autonomic, scalable, dynamic, and elegant. It is a complete system—and it works!

What Are the Risks?

By now it is probably becoming apparent that becoming samurai—becoming a Samurai Leader—is not going to be easy and it has its risks. Samurai can't just turn their back on a problem.

A SAMURAI STORY

A samurai by the name of Takagi got in an argument with three farmers in the neighborhood, was soundly beaten up out in the fields, and returned home. His wife said to him, "Haven't you forgotten about the matter of death?"

"Definitely not!" he replied.

His wife then retorted, "At any rate, a man dies only once. Of the various ways of dying— dying of disease, being cut down in battle, seppuku, or being beheaded—to die ignominiously would be a shame." She then went outside and was gone for a little while. When she returned, she carefully put the two children to bed, prepared some torches (for it was now dark), dressed herself for the battle, and then said, "When I went out a few moments ago to survey the scene, it seemed that the three men went into a place for a discussion. Now is the right time. Let's go quickly!"

So saying, they went out, burning torches and wearing short swords. They broke into their opponent's place and dispersed them, both husband and wife slashing about and killing two of the men and wounding the other. [2]

In this story, the wife (who is also samurai) knew what their code required. Armed with that knowledge, the appropriate action could be determined. With the conviction comes the courage to execute. There is power in knowing that one is doing the right thing. Becoming a Samurai Leader will increase one's power, but it will force issues that previously an individual might have preferred to ignore.

Here's why it is going to be worth it. Being a Samurai Leader will lead to:

- a bolder and more confident approach to work;
- a clearer stance on morally ambiguous issues;
- greater self-control;
- more respect from your peers;
- more respect from your workplace bosses;
- more respect from the people who work for you;
- a greater sense of connectedness;

and best of all

- you will be happier!

Actually, it gets even better than that, but that list all by itself is hard to believe. Yet, those are the benefits of committing one's actions to the right value system. It's not easy to do that, but it gets done one step at a time, one action at a time. And when you know the code, you know what action to take. Because the Samurai Code is so clear and definitive, as you commit your actions to it it all becomes more natural and as smooth and fluid as a sword stroke, with no hesitancy or second-guessing.

It's like the pivotal scene in the Tom Cruise movie *The Last Samurai* where Tom's character is learning how to fight with the sword. He keeps getting defeated in his learning exercises. He finally succeeds when he stops thinking his way through the fight and instead surrenders himself to the fight and becomes one with the sword. Hesitancy, doubt, and fear all disappear—he's "in the zone."

To be "in the zone" requires no confusion of mind, no behavioral doubt. When an athlete is "in the zone"—when Michael Jordan was red hot or when Tiger Woods has his "A" game working—there is no mental instruction going on, no considering of this choice or that. There is not a single doubt embedded in the consciousness, there is only a perfect clarity of purpose, a seamless linking of being and doing. And being "in the zone" isn't limited to athletes or warriors in battle—it's there for the manager negotiating an M&A transaction or giving a speech to an employee group or leading a staff meeting or confronting an unhappy customer or making a huge new sale.

Sword

Strokes

GETTING "IN THE ZONE"

Management can be fun. Leading a group of people to accomplish a common endeavor can be a terrific way to spend one's life. But a manager needs to have his "A" game most of the time.

For a manager to be "in the zone" a number of things have to come together:

- Belief that the skill set required to achieve the objective is available and harnessed
- "Seeing" the desired result and continuously communicating it to the team
- No doubts that it is the right thing to do
- A positive attitude, no negativity
- Joy in the doing of it

This requires acting in accordance with a true way of being. It can't be faked because one cannot successfully lie to oneself. Of course, it is not easy to achieve. No one is in the zone all the time. And even when in the zone, it doesn't mean one necessarily will make the right decision about whether to upgrade an HR system, buy a new piece of equipment, hire a new employee, or acquire a company. Mistakes will still be made, unforeseeable events will still occur. But managing in accordance with a way of being, one centered around a clear and comprehensive code of behavior that intuitively feels right and meets the needs of the day, will lead to better decision making. It will lead to employees sharing "the zone" with their manager!

When you're doing your best work, it will seem effortless!

"Are you telling me that a manager who acts in accordance with the Samurai Code—modified somewhat to meet present-day realities—will become a better manager, clearer of purpose, stronger in mind and body, and sometimes even 'in the zone'?"

That's right! Samurai Leaders operate "in the zone." That is what this book is offering. Pretty cool, isn't it?

Samurai Leaders Inspire Others

The true test of a leader is whether his or her words and deeds inspire others to maximize the right and necessary performance. In today's world, business leaders are constantly challenged to meet competitive and market threats. To fail to do so can have immediate disastrous consequences—falling market share, declining stock prices, and even bankruptcy and dissolution. On such a battleground, the Samurai Leader prevails.

A SAMURAI LEADER STORY

Gordon took over as CEO of Continental Airlines at a time when that airline was once again on the brink of bankruptcy and probable dissolution. As an industry veteran who had risen through the ranks, he understood better than anyone how important it was for an airline to have all of its employees working together. He also knew that he had to make a lot of changes very quickly if the airline was going to survive. The first thing he did was to bring in several highly trusted senior executives. He knew they would fight alongside him, ensure he had the best information possible, and ensure that the best options could be considered. From the prior executive ranks, he kept the best and most capable that he believed would stay the course with him in what was a very tough battle. Now with a team, he formulated a strategy that focused on the key success factors.

Then he rallied the troops and rallied the troops and rallied the troops and rallied the troops. In every appearance, in every presentation, he preached, "If you want to stay in the pizza business, sooner or later you have to deliver a good pizza." Focus on the basics! In operating an airline, one had to 1) Get people where they're going on time, 2) Get bags to arrive with the customers, and 3) Have airline employees that smile. He relentlessly preached the message—the same message—over and over again. He was out in front with the customers, in the cockpit with the pilots, in the galleys with the flight attendants, and out on the ramp with the mechanics and ground service employees. He faced every tough question and issue head on. He led from the front. He got everyone working together and focused on exactly what it would take to turn the airline around.

Importantly, one didn't need to look far to see what behavior was expected and required. All it took was to observe Gordon and his management team. Any manager whose actions didn't mirror the values didn't stay a manager. And the values were clear: work together, treat everyone with respect, no backing away from problems, no surrendering to the competition, do your best work every day, show the customers a smile and a caring attitude.

The battle wasn't won in a day. The airline had to fight from a long way back, and had to overcome myriad obstacles. Yet the team fought through it all, led by its leader who understood it took a team to win. He understood that if you couldn't be relied on, if you weren't willing to fight no matter how hard the battle, you couldn't be on the team. And that to harness the power of the team, the individual couldn't be emphasized, rewards had to be shared with everyone fairly, and no one could win unless everyone won.

The airline went from being one of the worst airlines in the world to being one of the best. The values that brought it through its darkest days are still the same values practiced every day.

It has an experienced and battle-hardened management team who work together. Its employees know what they have to do and they do it—smiling.

Anyone familiar with the Continental Airlines story knows that its CEO during its turnaround years was a reincarnation of a samurai warrior leader. His actions set the direction for everyone.

Sword

Strokes

LEADING BY EXAMPLE

Whether running a small department, a large division, or a whole company, it is essential that every member of that unit understands what they are supposed to do, how they are supposed to act, and the standards to which they will be held. Implicit in this is how the everyday work gets done. The leader must mirror the desired behavior. The employees will follow what is done much more than what is said. Moreover, the employees will look to the whole of their leaders' performance, not just the few characteristics that most managers would like to feature. Wise leaders know that *everything they do* is observed, every comment they make is overheard, every look on their face is scrutinized.

Leaders who won't listen to a customer's complaint will have customer service people who also don't listen. Leaders who are superior and abrupt to their employees set the tone for everyone else. Leaders who live lavishly on their expense accounts encourage all their sales people to cheat on theirs. Fortunately, the opposite is also true. Leaders who care for their employees and their customers will have employees who care for each other and take care of their customers. Leaders who are honest and hardworking will drive those attributes in others. The leader's whole character is at issue. It sets the standards of behavior for everyone. With every promotion, a manager's character is more exposed.

Employees can be ruthless imitators.

When the leader is strong, visible, and acts consistently to a clear set of values, his or her actions create a multiplier effect that drives all of the other managers and employees to act consistently with those values. That creates an optimum management environment because it empowers all in the management group to make the tough and courageous decisions necessary to succeed—so long as they are acting in accordance with the values. The following story is a perfect example.

A SAMURAI LEADER STORY

Bonnie, Senior Vice President of Marketing and Sales for Continental Airlines, had a big problem—a forty-million-dollar problem. Continental, under Bonnie's guidance, had developed a new technology tool for Continental to use with its large corporate customers. It monitored and measured the booking patterns, policy performance, and value creation of the relationship. With the technology in place, the customer's real-time data could be applied to determine the return on investment for both Continental and the customer of the discounted fares, inventory management preferences, travel upgrades, and other benefits that were provided to the customer.

Bonnie and her team had gone to all their large corporate customers and explained the mutual benefits of using this new tool. After initial objection, almost all of the customers saw the benefit and went along with Continental's requirement that it be a part of any preferred customer agreement.

But one of Continental's largest customers, a major Fortune 500 company doing $40 million a year with Continental, didn't want to use the new technology. They wanted the continuation of their discounts and the other benefits of the relationship without the improved accountability provided by the new tool.

Continental had told all of its other corporations that using the new application was a requirement for the discounts, etc., and now was faced with one of its largest customers saying "no!" Negotiations went on for a while, trying to break the impasse, but with no resolution. Now Bonnie had to decide what to do.

It is not easy walking away from a $40 million customer, but Bonnie knew that using this new technology application was the right way to do business. She knew that all her other large customers had gone along with this business process change because she had said it would be part of any deal Continental would do going forward. She felt she had no choice.

The right business decision was to end the relationship with that customer. So, she did it.

Final note: That particular customer relationship was lost for several years. But Continental's profitability on its corporate business improved—thanks, in part, to utilization of that new technology. Bonnie won the prestigious Laurels Award for outstanding achievement in using technology for change in business practices and Continental consistently took top awards for being the favorite airline of corporate travel managers.

It is not irrelevant to Bonnie's story that she had Gordon for her boss. Her decision was consistent with the principles of Gordon's approach to management. And those were her principles, as well. Continental would feel the pain of losing that customer, but making tough decisions like that also made Continental stronger.

Being samurai is infectious. Gordon's being samurai brings out Bonnie's samurai nature, which flows down through her organization.

It should also be noted that several different samurai characteristics were involved in Bonnie's actions. First, she had led the development of new technology by facing up to a problem that everyone else in the industry had previously ignored. Then she had fought through the initial customer resistance. Lastly, when opposed by a dissenting major customer, she kept her pledge to, and the trust of, her other customers. Not surprisingly, within Continental she was highly respected for her clear thinking and the boldness of her actions.

The holistic approach to a way of acting is samurai. All of one's actions are inseparably inter-connected. Compliance with the Code wasn't just for sometimes or when they were in battle or when they were "at work." Similarly, distinguishing between a way of being when at work versus a way of being during one's personal life would seem nonsense to a samurai. How could someone be two different people?

A person has only one way of being. That way of being is a composite of many characteristics. The more these characteristics are consistent and promote a positive nature, the stronger the individual becomes. Courage without honor, ambition without compassion, intelligence without honesty, aggressive-ness without loyalty—all are hazardous combina-tions over the course of a lifetime. They sow seeds of distrust and discontent.

In contrast, greatness in an individual invariably included combinations of the samurai traits. Lincoln was courageous, compassionate, and wise. Washington was a warrior of rectitude, self-discipline, and loyalty. Our heroes are rarely one dimensional.

QUESTIONS TO CONSIDER

1. When have you felt you were being a really good leader? Were you "in the zone?" What personal characteristics were you exhibiting?

2. What leaders have you admired? Did they have any common traits?

3. Why do you think the United States Marines have a code? Is it important to the way they perform in battle? To their daily activities?

CHAPTER TWO

THE CODE OF THE SAMURAI
PART I:
HONOR, COURAGE, RECTITUDE, LOYALTY

The next two chapters present the basic elements of the Code of the Samurai. You'll see why and how they are the foundation for building a successful career. Later chapters will show how to integrate samurai behaviors into day-to-day business decisions. Most of what is presented is not difficult to understand, but it is not intuitive at first. But once you "get it," it will all fall into place easily.

Much of what is presented here is in a battle-oriented context. This is not to suggest that business is only about fighting. Getting to "win-win" through cooperation and teamwork, helping others, and self-sacrifice can be hugely important. Yet, when it comes right down to it, one must act aggressively—and there is a right way to do that!

The use of war metaphors in business happens all the time. Business and war are viewed by many to have so much in common that texts on the conduct of wars are often read as guides on how to do business (e.g., Sun Tzu's *The Art of War*). Certainly it would be naive to think that any code for managers could preach a passive and benign set of standards. Business requires a warrior spirit and a code meant for warriors.

First and foremost, the Code of the Samurai is a warrior's code. It evolved over the course of five hundred years to instruct samurai how to behave and prevail during the extended periods of clan-against-clan warfare, which were the dominating events of Japan's feudal history. However, because samurai came to compose a social class, the code also evolved to address daily behavior. It guides the samurai's behavior holistically during times of both peace and war, while in a social environment as well as when on the battlefield. Because it is a warrior's code, it can be quite rigid. Battles could be won or lost based on the calm thinking of its generals and on whether the combatants fight or flee. Because of its roots in Zen Buddhism, it focuses on right actions and the connectedness of all things. **Though at first these two drivers (a code for peace and a code for war) may be viewed as being mutually antagonistic, they are in fact mutually supportive.**

This leads us to the first element of the Samurai Leader Code.

Honor

What is honor, anyway—and does anybody care? People don't talk about it much. It seems sort of an outmoded concept, something out of nineteenth-century romanticism. In the corporate world, does acting honorably mean anything? Management evaluation forms don't evaluate managers based on it. Why? It's not just a matter of honesty or integrity (although that gets closer to it)—it's just believed that in business, situations do not come up that often that test one's sense of honor.

Or do they? Is a manager acting honorably when:

- he ignores commitments made to customers or clients
- he badmouths his own company
- he misrepresents or withholds important information
- he blames someone else for his mistake
- he takes out his anger on his subordinates
- he abuses his power
- he doesn't stand up for others who need his help

Honor seems to be one of those elusive qualities that doesn't really tie to any one action but can sum up a person's whole way of being. It's Atticus Finch in *To Kill a Mockingbird*, it's Rick at the end of *Casablanca*. Neither Atticus nor Rick would ever do as a manager any of the things mentioned earlier.

For a samurai, honor is the overarching guide to right actions. It is infused into every element of the Samurai Code.

A SAMURAI STORY

Once when Fukuchi Rokurouemon was leaving the castle, the palanquin (a covered litter supported by poles carried on men's shoulders) of an upper class woman was passing by. A samurai who was standing there made the proper salutation. A halberd (a weapon with an ax-like blade and a steel spike mounted on a long pole) carrier who was with the palanquin procession, however, said to the samurai that he did not bow low enough and struck him on the head with the handle of his halberd.

When the samurai wiped his head, he found that he was bleeding. In just that condition he stood up and said, "You have committed an outrageous act, even though I was courteous. A regrettable piece of luck." So saying, he cut the halberd carrier down with a single blow.

Rokurouemon unsheathed his sword, stood before the samurai, and said, "Put away your sword. Within the castle grounds it is forbidden to go about holding a naked blade."

The man said, "What happened now was unavoidable, and I was compelled by the circumstances. Certainly, you could see that this was so. Although I would like to sheath my sword, it is difficult to do so due to the tone of your words. It is unpleasant, but I shall be glad to accept your challenge."

Rokurouemon immediately threw down his sword and said courteously, "What you have said is reasonable. I will bear witness that your conduct was quite admirable. I will back you up even if it means forfeiting my own life. Now put away your sword."

"With pleasure," the man said, and sheathed his sword.

On being asked where he was from, the samurai replied that he was a retainer of Lord Tako Nagato. Therefore, Rokurouemon accompanied him and explained the circumstances. Knowing that the woman in the palanquin was the wife of a nobleman, however, Lord Nagato ordered his retainer to commit seppuku (hara-kiri, killing oneself by stabbing a knife into one's abdomen).

Rokurouemon came forward and said, "Because I have given the promise of a samurai, if this man is ordered to commit seppuku, then I will commit seppuku first."

It is said the affair was thus finished without mishap and no one was punished for it. [3]

The beauty of this samurai story is that it unfolds almost like a dance, with each of the samurai involved understanding and relying upon the other to take the appropriate actions. They could do so because they knew they shared the Code of the Samurai. Had they not trusted each other when first they met, one would have ended up killing the other.

How much more productive would managers be if they too shared a code with their peers to always behave honorably? The costs of dealing with the issues of lack of trust are incredibly high. Many potentially valuable business deals crash because the parties never quite trust each other.

Sword

Strokes

ESTABLISHING TRUST

The trust problem in business is that everyone starts with the assumption that no one can be trusted. Everyone has been burned in the past when they trusted someone. So all business dealings become a matter of contract and the handshake at the time of signing the contract is essentially meaningless. This produces several major problems:

- The contract has to cover all possible eventualities—which no contract realistically can.
- Good deals get lost in needless fighting over contract terms.
- Relationships sour during the contract negotiations.

This is not to say that contracts aren't necessary or that major terms don't need to be negotiated. But ultimately few contracts can bridge parties that don't trust each other. Unless the business situation is a "one time only, get in and get out" kind of deal, many terms in a contract are better off being left vague rather than being fiercely fought over. Leave the problem for the future and trust that a healthy business relationship will resolve it. Most likely the circumstances then will be different than anticipated.

A good leader knows that the best business relationships exist at the personal level. A manager should not be afraid to be the first one to trust. The handshake should never be minimalized. More managers will bend over backwards to meet a personalized handshake commitment than will do so if only a contract right is at issue.

Few managers survive a reputation for being untrustworthy!

Why Is Honor Important?

For a samurai, acting in an honorable manner required actions consistent with the Way of the Samurai. Here again, all the elements of the code come together to compose a way of being. It was not just a matter of avoiding being shamed by one's action or insisting on a duel if one was deemed to have been insulted. If that were all it took, maintaining one's honor would be something only occasionally challenged—and it wouldn't be that significant.

The reality of honor is something more. It's trying to do the right thing all the time. It's ignoring one's fears and persevering in the face of all challenges in order to do what needs to be done. It's self-sacrificing when the needs of others are paramount. It's going through every day without taking moral shortcuts. It's keeping all one's promises whether convenient or not. It's doing what one says one is going to do no matter how much more difficult or burdensome than originally anticipated.

A samurai recognized that everyday behavior was an important measure of a man. A samurai was careful of his appearance. It would shame them if their clothing were slovenly or if they were unkempt. A samurai was taught that gossiping about others was inappropriate and shamed the one spreading gossip. Secrets were to be kept. In matters both little and large, the discipline of always acting correctly led samurai to be honored.

It is no different for a manager. If a manager wants the respect of his coworkers, he or she needs to be aware that it is earned or lost every single day. It is a matter of holding oneself to high standards of behavior that relate to every facet of day-to-day experience and then living to those standards. It's "walking the talk." It's "standing up to the challenge."

In our cynical world, too many believe that the price of honor is too costly. When confronted by a challenge where the honorable action seems to promise immediate disadvantages, the honorable action is forsaken. One ignores that inner voice that anguishes over moral shortcuts and political convenience. The irony is that the costs of acting dishonorably are much too high.

- "Of men who have a sense of honor, more come through alive than are slain, but from those who flee comes neither glory nor any help." (Homer, *The Iliad*)
- "Count it the greatest sin to prefer life to honor, and for the sake of living to lose what makes life worth having." (Juvenal, *Satires*)
- "Mine honor is my life; both grow in one; Take honor from me, and my life is done." (Shakespeare, *King Richard II*)
- "For what is a man profited, if he shall gain the whole world, and lose his own soul." (The Book of Matthew)

Over time, everyone seems to know who acts honorably and who does not. They are identified without even having to do anything extraordinary. Their way of being stands out clearly amidst the fog of confused and abused personalities. They are a beacon to others who are looking for guidance. Most people really do want to do the right thing, they are just afraid. They need a leader.

A SAMURAI LEADER STORY

Mike, a client executive with IBM, was in a battle with his largest customer and he was losing. The fight was over the technical superiority and pricing of the core operating system. The customer was arguing that other technology solutions had surpassed IBM's and that IBM's pricing was far too high given the business conditions in the marketplace. The customer was all set to walk away from its relationship with IBM. Mike would lose an account worth over $200 million in revenue over the next couple of years.

Mike's relationship with the customer was excellent and he understood very well the basis for the customer's point of view. He also knew that IBM's technology offering really was the best solution for the client. But the equation underpinning the pricing really had become too skewed in IBM's favor, based on a historical monopoly-like position. The pricing was too high.

But the pricing issue was very complicated because it was license based and a lot of other companies were paying at the quoted price and IBM did not want to give up its profit margin on the technology to anyone, lest they end up losing it to everyone.

Mike knew he needed help—mostly within IBM—or this customer would be lost. So, he did a very smart thing. He convened a meeting with the customer's leadership team and the IBM executives that had the power to change the limitations under which he was working. Based on relationships that had been building for several years, the meeting was conducted by both sides on a basis that was very open and honest. By the end of the meeting, several of the principals made personal commitments to work through the issues.

The differences weren't resolved quickly. Mike was at the center of all these negotiations, continually using the trust that both sides had in him to ensure that issues continued to be honestly and openly discussed. It took months more of work, but by the end it was all worth it.

Instead of having the customer walk away, IBM signed a vastly expanded agreement with the customer than had previously existed. A much bigger relationship now was in place that could be used as a model for doing business going forward. The new agreement was worth over $430 million to IBM.

Mike could never have succeeded without his acting in several ways characteristic of a samurai.

- First, he assessed the situation critically and sought out allies when he saw he needed help to win the battle.
- He encouraged open and honest dialogue and maintained everyone's trust while having access to highly confidential information and materials.
- He continually fought through the business issues when more than once the deal was close to being killed off by one or the other of the parties.
- He tried his best to do the right thing for both parties and his actions at all times reflected his sense of honor.

It made the difference.

Earning Honor

Too many managers are unmindful of the accumulated effect of minor actions, and so never understand why they are not respected—are not honored. They think that all their little managerial sins will be forgiven if they make their numbers or sign up the big deals. They forget that getting the small things right makes getting the big things done more likely. They forget that over time no one makes their numbers all the time and that there are dry spells when no big deals get signed up. It is during these times when those who act honorably all the time get the advantage. They are the ones who are respected; they are the trusted ones.

Most non-samurai managers know that all good relationships are founded on respect. They just don't know how to get it. They don't believe that honor matters. They can't see the link between honor and respect. A Samurai Leader cannot separate himself from his honor.

An interesting characteristic of honor is that it can be contagious. Think of the expression, "It's an honor to meet you." That statement suggests that when dealing with honorable people, mere association confers honor on others. And it is true. When around honorable people, there is an urge to rise to their standard. A Samurai Leader, managing a department in accordance with the Code, will inspire his or her employees to improve their behavior. It is a truth that one wants the respect of those one respects.

To a samurai, the short-term benefits of acting without honor could not outweigh the long-term disadvantages. No fortress can be built on a weak foundation; in times of stress, it always collapses. Over a lifetime, the costs of living without honor are devastating. Success sours and then disappears. Samurai Leaders know this.

QUESTIONS TO CONSIDER

1. If you acted dishonorably in the past, was it worth it?

2. Whom do you know that you would describe as being very honorable? How is that person generally regarded?

Courage and a Warrior Spirit

You knew this was part of it. And maybe this one seems the hardest. But don't confuse courage with fearlessness (which is the subject of future chapters). Courage only requires that you do what you know you need to do, even though you're afraid. (But don't worry, we'll deal with the fear problem too.)

Courage isn't that unusual. Our soldiers, ordinary men and women, show courage every day. When was it decided that a good manager didn't need it? Who holds that delusion? A business person spends every day on a battlefield; a battlefield of warring companies, competing business plans, struggling departments, and voracious egos.

The need for a warrior spirit is pretty obvious too. When you live on a battlefield, you have to be ready to fight. You have to be willing to attack. A true samurai always wanted to be at the front of the charge against the enemy. And if he died in battle, he wanted his body to lie facing the front.

A SAMURAI STORY

TWO LITTLE STORIES FROM THE SEVENTEENTH CENTURY

In China, there once was a man who liked pictures of dragons, and his clothing and furnishings were all designed accordingly. His deep affection for dragons was brought to the attention of the dragon god, and one day a real dragon appeared before his window. It is said he died of fright. He was probably a man who always spoke big words but acted differently when facing the real thing.

At a great conference, a certain samurai explained his dissenting opinion and said that he was resolved to kill the conference leader if it were not accepted. His motion was passed. After the procedures were over, the samurai said, "Their assent came quickly. I think they are too weak and unreliable to be counselors to the master." [4]

TWO SAMURAI LEADER STORIES

A few years ago, SystemOne Corporation was facing losing its largest customer to Sabre, even though there was a contractual relationship holding them together. Sabre was offering a much more attractive deal that SystemOne couldn't match. Bill, the general counsel of SystemOne, met with the customer's general counsel, and informed him that he had hired a plaintiff's litigation law firm known for being very good and very aggressive. He planned to bring a tortious interference with contract lawsuit against Sabre if necessary to keep the customer from switching away.

The customer's general counsel was out-raged and exclaimed, "That law firm is a pack of mad dogs! They attack! Attack! Attack!"

"Yes," Bill replied. "But they are my mad dogs!"

The customer stayed with SystemOne.

A large South American airline, a major distributor of the goods and services of SystemOne, wanted to get out of their partnership agreement with SystemOne. They claimed that SystemOne was in breach of certain terms and conditions of that agreement as a result of the sale of SystemOne to a new party. The CEO of the airline came to meet with Bill, now the CEO of SystemOne, and each side was represented by its lawyers. The airline's lawyers were very confident that their side was in the right and that they would prevail in a lawsuit. If they lost, their clients financial exposure would be very large. Yet, they were very confident of victory.

Bill listened to the lawyers wrangling over the issues for a while, then he turned to the airline CEO and said, "You've got very good lawyers here...and they are probably right, you very well could win in court. After all, they are very good lawyers...although my lawyers are good, too. But ask your lawyers right now whether they will guarantee you that they will win. Will they guarantee it? Of course, they won't—they can't. A court—a jury's decision—isn't that predictable." He paused for a moment and looked around the room.

Then Bill continued, "But I'll guarantee you something. I guarantee that if you try to get out of our agreement, I guarantee that I will fight this all the way, I will take you to court, and I won't stop fighting. Your lawyers know me. Ask them whether they doubt that at all."

The airline's lawyers knew Bill, both personally and by reputation, and they nodded that that was true.

The airline's CEO stood up. "I understand. We won't try to get out of the agreement."

Displaying a warrior approach to customers and distributors is not usually the best way to deal with them. It is much better to build the relationship by providing superior products and service. But sometimes it is not about product and services and sometimes too much is at risk to not fight. It is then that having a reputation as a warrior can be a great help. It may in fact prevent a fight from ever starting. It's not smart to pick on a warrior.

Sword

Strokes

DON'T BE A VICTIM

The hardest battles to fight are the ones you know you are going to lose. In chapter 4, we'll discuss more on choosing and fighting battles. But for the purpose here, the key is recognizing that sometimes you have to fight when you don't have a chance of winning. The reason for fighting these battles is to avoid being victimized.

Victimization occurs because predators always attack the weak. That is as true in the business world as it is in the jungle. If a manager is perceived as unwilling to fight necessary battles, then over time, managers that are more aggressive will take what they want. Sometimes it is even better to lose a battle than to win it. It can raise the competition's cost of doing business, exhaust their resources, and divert their attention from what really matters.

Competitors, whether internal or external, must be taught that nothing can be taken from a Samurai Leader that will not be hard-fought—not even little things. The aggressive predators will go somewhere else that will not be as difficult.

The Courage to Create Change

In many cases, the fight a manager needs to wage is not against anyone, but rather against "the way things are." This type of battle can be the most daunting and requires true courage. However, business can grant huge rewards to those who swim against popular currents and succeed.

SAMURAI LEADER STORY

Back in the early 1990s, FedEx chairman and founder Fred Smith became very interested in how to improve the quality of the service network his company operated every night. Too often packages were lost or weren't delivered on time, billing was incorrect, and customers weren't satisfied. The senior executive team was taken off site and given a weekend course by a leading quality consultant. Fred's key managers were then injected back into the company equipped with exciting new ideas and a game plan to work out test programs in a couple of key areas.

Two years later, very little had changed. The whole subject had fallen on painful disinterest. Fred's managers believed that the processes required to deliver packages all over the world, door to door, and overnight were complicated and would fail sometimes. It couldn't be improved.

Tom, the senior vice president of sales and customer service, didn't buy it. He came to believe that something had been missed in the quality improvement strategy. The strategy was too "small" in its conception and didn't build enough support from departmental leaders to overcome the very powerful "conventional wisdom."

Tom's biggest problem was that the first try had failed and everyone knew it. Many managers were reluctant to try again. They felt it would be a waste of time and would reflect badly on them when once again it didn't work. He was advised by others to just let things remain as they were. It wasn't that bad. For Tom "not that bad" wasn't near good enough.

Tom determined to totally change the one group over of which he had nearly complete control: the customer service team that answered almost 200,000 phone calls every day from customers.

The transformation started with a secret retreat in North Carolina where they mapped out the many processes and examined all the interconnections where frequent delivery and billing failures occurred. By the end of the meeting, they were committed to scrutinizing all the inter-connected processes they directly controlled. And Tom had a new mission: convince one other senior vice president to do the same with his division.

Managers were encouraged to let go of old perceptions and old practices, to see things as they really were, and to not be afraid to admit to problems. Rather than seeing functions as separate and individual, they came to see the functions as inter-related. Everything was connected.

Heroes emerged in department after department as people first understood, then applied, then innovated using new insights into the weaknesses and opportunities of their various processes. Cycle times in certain operations were cut by 90 percent with error rates dropping to a small fraction of the earlier "best practice" results.

Based on Tom and his team's success, the FedEx CEO put the whole company on the same track. As part of the process, a much more comprehensive measure of the company's service was put in place. It encompassed virtually every employee. The results were astounding. Within twelve months, the absolute number of "failure points" had dropped by 30 percent, even though total packages handled had risen by 35 percent! More importantly, the

*annual employee survey of management leader-
ship had improved to the highest level ever
recorded, and the company's profit margin had
improved significantly.*

*The following year, Fred Smith and his key
management team were honored in Washington,
DC, as FedEx became the first-ever American
service corporation to win the coveted Malcolm
Baldrige National Quality Award.*

The FedEx story is notable for several reasons. As
will often be the case, to succeed the manager (Tom)
needed to fight established belief, he needed to redi-
rect his team and attack the problem holistically, and
he had to excite the troops who actually did the day-
to-day work. With success, the culture of the company evolved to incorporate the new learnings, both
process specific and behavioral. Tom's samurai characteristics took root in the company—a company naturally fertile for such ideas because of its leadership.

As the FedEx story demonstrates, in not all
instances where courage is required is there an actual
battle. In fact, courage is a constant and an everyday
necessity for a Samurai Leader. Courage is required to
confront issues head-on, to deal with difficult people,
to accept defeats without running away and hiding, to
take risks that have substantial downsides. The list of

events that will require courage from a leader over the course of a career is almost endless.

So, get used to it! The more you step up to the plate and swing the bat, the easier it gets. Not swinging the bat is not an option! In the long run, not ever swinging the bat is fatal! But the good news is, just like the Cowardly Lion in the *Wizard of Oz,* all the courage you will ever need is already inside of you. The courage you think you lack is a direct consequence of giving too much importance to things that you perceive as being threats. As will be shown here, there is no bogeyman in most of those closets! And the ones that do exist, you can deal with.

You'll see!

QUESTIONS TO CONSIDER

1. How do you explain the courage shown by so many ordinary people when facing terminal illnesses, natural disasters, and wartime?

2. What have you done where you demonstrated true courage?

Rectitude: Acting Wisely and Correctly

To a samurai, courage without reason is like an arrow without a bow. Life is about doing the right thing and knowing when to do it. As stated in a well-known quote on the Samurai Code, "Rectitude is the power of deciding upon a certain course of conduct in accordance with reason, without wavering—to die when it is right to die, to strike when to strike is right."

For a samurai there were many requirements to the concept of correct behavior. All actions had to be considered against the strictures of the whole of the Code. This necessitated acting intelligently and without self-interest. Moreover, his actions had to take into account the duty he owed his master (employer), the duty he owed to his family, and the duty he owed to others he encountered. A samurai believed that if he acted wisely and well, he would not only succeed in his personal ambitions, but would also be rewarded in his next life for his exemplary behavior—hopefully by coming back again as a samurai.

It was understood that in order to act with rectitude, one should take advantage of guidance from others. Yamamoto Tsunetomo, a seventeenth-century samurai and author of *Hagakure,* one of the most revered texts on samurai, stated this point beautifully:

Because we do most things relying on our own sagacity we become self-interested, turn our backs on reason, and things do not turn out well. As seen by other people, this is sordid, weak, narrow, and inefficient. When one is not capable of true intelligence, it is good to consult with someone of good sense. An advisor will fulfill the Way when he makes a decision by selfless and frank intelligence because he is not personally involved. This way of doing things will certainly be seen by others as being strongly rooted. It is, for example, like a large tree with many roots. One man's intelligence is like a tree that has just been stuck in the ground....

We learn about the sayings and deeds of the men of old in order to entrust ourselves to their wisdom and prevent selfishness. When we throw off our own bias, follow the sayings of the ancients, and confer with other people, matters should go well and without mishap.[5]

There is much in what is written in this passage to guide a Samurai Leader. In a modern corporation, it is hard for an individual manager to succeed who only thinks selfishly and does not take advantage of the wisdom and experience of others. A tree nourished and supported by many roots is going to fare much better in any forest.

Putting It in Action

"Wait a minute—Does this rectitude thing in the code mean that to be a Samurai Leader I've got to do the morally right thing...Not be selfish...Listen to others...and be a good teammate? That's the same stuff my mom told me! What do I need this book for?"

We're not overly confused about what the right values are. **It's putting them into practice that seems to be the problem!** Moreover, too many managers seem to think that "doing the right thing" all the time will hold them back in their careers or keep them from making the most money possible. So, rather than lose the big bucks, they lose the values.

A SAMURAI LEADER STORY

Once there was a business that had entered a period of decline. In years earlier, it was a brand name that had created a new industry, the family roadside motel.

Over time, the founder had retired, and his visions were lost. Professional managers took over, people who valued the current financial numbers more than the interests of their ultimate customers, the traveling public. Soon other hotel brands were emerging that embodied better value and greater accessibility. The market share of the best-known family hotel brand began to decline, slowly, and then more rapidly.

The corporate managers realized the trap. They couldn't revitalize the brand without cutting profits. They couldn't flood the market with new properties because franchisee interests could turn into an intense, costly legal battle.

A clever new CFO piled a huge amount of debt onto the company and then paid out a huge cash dividend (greater than the then stock price, actually). Now the company was reduced to a highly leveraged commodity ready for sale. And sold it was, to a British company, right before the first Gulf War and ensuing recession. It was a terrible time to pay a high price for a globally known brand name with such a weak capital structure and tarnished assets.

Management under the new owner did what it could to deal with the problem, but the financial markets in the UK demanded profits to justify the acquisition. More poor properties were added to the brand. The service spiral in the minds of customers worsened.

The situation required revolution. It required courage and conviction about the importance of the ultimate customer.

Tom was recruited as the new CEO. Coming from a world where the importance of customer service and customer satisfaction was paramount, he plotted a new course. A revolutionary change in corporate strategy would cut profits initially, not increase them. And an extended period of negative results would be the end of Tom's career.

Tom came to believe he had to take the risk. So, he went to work! He started by building a new brand team, often using talented people that had been frustrated in the previous environment. Long-time franchising experts and global marketers were blended with new recruits bringing real estate development skills and service management knowledge. A wholly new strategic plan was developed that charted a bold course to revitalize the company and its properties. It was a very big bet!

To introduce their plan, a watershed speech was developed for delivery at the next worldwide convention of franchisees, a meeting of three thousand people who had widely varying interests in the next stages of the brand's development. The speech was just as critical in selling the new approach to the parent company management and its board, because they would be in attendance and would be powerfully affected by the reaction of the audience.

As Tom walked onto the stage, it was clear to him that a new confidence in the company's direction was essential. What he knew was that people would follow a courageous captain, suffer hardships, and steel themselves for sacrifice if they believed in the cause and the leadership. What he knew was that fixing the image of the brand was the right thing to do for both the shareholders and the customers. It was what had to be done—no matter how difficult.

Step by step, both the importance of change and the rationale for a new course were outlined in inspiring terms. The hard reality of a new environment, where properties either would be shaped up or would be shipped out, was laid down as immutable planks in the new strategy. The value of quality and customer satisfaction were emphasized again and again as Tom related example after example of the success of companies that valued their customers first and their profit returns second.

In the end, even though most in the audience realized that they might get caught in the crossfire of brand improvement and the cynical ones thought that it was probably just lip service, the audience erupted in standing applause. They realized that what was said about the dishonesty of the past was true, and that ultimately they would all lose from following the past strategy. They realized that the painful process of improvement would bring better financial returns as the value of the brand in the market place was again polished and marketed.

Brand preference numbers and consumer satisfaction scores began to rise slowly for the first time in a decade, and then faster, ultimately improving by more than 50 percent. Disgruntled franchisees dropped out as their properties were forced out through the contractual quality requirements, and the association leadership began to take a tough line themselves with the brands and with the owners. Most importantly, the "brand power" index, relating the share of the brand's revenue in the category to its share of rooms, climbed year after year for five straight years, ultimately generating over $1 billion in added profits for both the hotel and brand owners.

Tom and his team had done it. With steadfast determination to "do the right thing," they had turned Holiday Inn International around.

Executive management in Britain realized the importance of customer satisfaction, and single-minded focus on the hotel market. It divested itself of its nonhotel interests. Another major brand, InterContinental Hotels, was acquired, and the resulting global hotel power-house was reborn as the InterContinental Hotels Group. Holiday Inn, the brand that started it all, was back on the path to market leadership.

Remember, too, that this isn't just about doing the moral thing—that's only half of it. You still have to get the business decision right! Fighting a battle with the wrong strategy is not a ticket to success no matter how virtuous one is. This book is aimed at making a manager's actions wiser—the goal is to improve decision making, not just shrink the number of managers with legal problems. (Future chapters are aimed at reframing how a manager needs to think about things.) One could better describe it as "Doing the right thing right." As the Holiday Inn story demonstrates, sometimes a business leader must face hard realities where not all the interested parties can equally be satisfied. The right course of action will make some people unhappy. It is most clear in such circumstances that business decisions reached with rectitude and wisdom will best confront the challenges—and they are the ones that will be viewed by most concerned parties as legitimate and necessary.

GETTING PLANS RIGHT

Companies are continuously involved in making plans. There are strategic plans, operating plans, sales plans, profit plans, and a host of other plans. Huge amounts of time are spent putting together these plans. So much of that time is wasted! It's wasted for the following reasons:

- the plans aren't based on available resources—they assume capabilities that don't exist;
- the people that have to execute the plan don't adequately participate in the plan creation;
- the planning process is too political; and
- no one looks at the plan after it is created.

This is pretty basic stuff! It's not rocket science. The only reason it is included here is that in most companies, in most plans, one or more of the mistakes outlined above is made regularly!

The lesson here is simple: Remember Management 101! Get the basics right.

QUESTIONS TO CONSIDER

1. When you have a problem, whom do you go to for advice? Why that person? (Of course, it depends on the problem, but work with this!)

2. Should people come to you for advice? Why?

The Duty of Loyalty

Unless a samurai was a ronin, loyalty to the *daimyo* (the lord of the territory) was an absolute. The daimyo's rights over the lives of his samurai were so complete that without any justification at all he could tell a samurai to perform any function, to become a monk, or even to kill himself. The samurai's sense of loyalty and duty was so complete that he would do whatever was requested—without challenge.

In the world of today, such ideas of loyalty and duty seem absurd. Yet, when life and death are on the line, even in today's cynical world, soldiers do show extraordinary loyalty to their platoon, to their battlefield commanders, and to their country. Policemen and firemen also show great loyalty to their comrades. So the idea of loyalty hasn't disappeared, nor its practice. But the question of to whom it is owed is much more a question of circumstances.

Once upon a time, managers felt real loyalty to the companies they worked for. And in most cases, they believed their company matched their loyalty to the company with the company's loyalty to them. But that was once upon a time; it is no longer the case.

A long history of layoffs; the reduction of benefits such as termination assistance, healthcare, and pensions; and the increased job mobility at every level of the organization has gradually killed off most managers' sense of personal identification with their company and minimized any sense of loyalty. The matter of loyalty to the company where one works seems to most managers to be an anachronism—no longer relevant to one's career planning.

A SAMURAI STORY

One of the most famous samurai exploits occurred in 1702 and is known as the story of the Forty-Seven Ronin. An important daimyo named Asano was staying at the shogun's court. While there, he had to take certain lessons in etiquette from a politically powerful and wealthy samurai named Kira. Dissatisfied with the presents Asano gave him for the lessons, Kira regularly criticized and ridiculed Asano. Finally, Asano could take the insults no longer and drew his sword and wounded Kira. As drawing a sword in the shogun's palace was strictly forbidden, Asano was ordered to commit seppuku, which he did, leaving his samurai retainers masterless ronin. They swore vengeance against Kira—who took precautions against being attacked by them.

The leader of these ronin was a samurai named Oishi Yoshio, a man who took the Bushido code very seriously. Knowing that Kira's forces outmanned them, Oishi went to great lengths to appear that he and the other ronin were no longer a threat to Asano. He even exaggerated his drinking and carousing to look as if he had forgotten his dead master and had become someone who could be safely ignored. Months passed in this way. Kira let down his guard. Then one snowy night, Oishi assembled the other forty-six ronin—all who had been secretly awaiting their chance for revenge—and they attacked Kira's fortress-like mansion. They outfought Kira's guards and they killed Kira. They took Kira's head and laid it at Asano's tomb.

These events concerned the shogun, as he had been trying to revive the samurai spirit following *the weakening effects of almost a century of peace. The deed of the forty-seven samurai was popularly viewed as a demonstration of true samurai honor and loyalty. However, their actions had been in violation of the law, which ultimately had to be followed. The shogun ordered Oishi and the other forty-five samurai (one had died in the fight) to commit suicide. They all acted honorably in their deaths. Their graves are still honored today out of respect for their samurai virtue.*

Personal relationships among individuals in business are often not easy to analyze. Most "friends" are really just acquaintances that disappear as soon as the business relationship disappears. For this reason if no other, the question of to which individuals does one owe loyalty is a difficult one. But demonstrating loyalty to the right individuals can have a profound impact on one's career. There are business managers out there who value it above everything else. The matter of loyalty is truly a two-edged sword.

There is no easy way to determine when one should demonstrate loyalty—or the extent to which one should go. And the Code of the Samurai does not set out parameters and conditions and rules and requirements. It never does. The facts and the circumstances govern.

A SAMURAI LEADER STORY

The CEO of SystemOne Corporation had structured a buyout of the company. It involved creating a joint venture with EDS, Continental Airlines, and Amadeus (which was owned by Lufthansa, Air France, and Iberia). He believed that the deal was necessary for the survival of his company and he entrusted Caren, the general counsel of SystemOne, with the challenge of leading the negotiation team and getting the transaction done. The CEO and Caren had worked together closely for years and he had confidence that even though the deal was very complicated and the other parties very difficult to deal with, Caren would make it happen.

Caren hated the deal and did not believe it was necessary for the survival of their company. She loved the company as it was and knew that the joint venture would forever alter the special environment that had been created there. She also believed that once the deal was done, she'd be out of her job and forced to leave the company after years of working her way up to become a vice president.

The deal took months to do, most of it spent in a law office conference room far away from

Caren's home and her new husband. The day after day negotiating from early morning to late at night, often going more than twenty-four hours without sleep, was mentally and emotionally arduous and physically draining. The deal was like dealing with the United Nations—numerous competing interests, countries and cultures, and personalities were involved. As the lead negotiator for her company and the business manager most responsible for the deal, Caren had no respite, no relief. She was fatigued, drained, and missed her home and husband. It was so tempting to not work through any one of the key issues, of which there were so many, and instead just let the deal die. No one would have even known; no one could blame her.

The problem that Caren couldn't get over was that her boss had trusted her to get it done. They had always backed each other up, always been there for the other. And she knew the other employees who knew about the deal were looking to her as well. So, she kept at it, kept fighting through the seemingly endless issues every day. Then one day, finally, it was done. The deal was signed.

As things worked out, things did change with the new management structure and, as Caren foresaw, the company's headquarters *were moved to a different state and she eventually had to leave the company. But elsewhere, things worked out for her. Samurai managers are in short supply and what they bring to companies is highly sought after. She discovered that many of the companies she had come in contact with wanted to hire her.*

And of course, she and the CEO are still extremely close. (She is also still happily married—samurai make good mates as well!)

To Whom Do You Owe Loyalty?

"Okay, I get it. Loyalty is important. I knew that. But to whom? Do I have to be loyal to the company I work for? They aren't going to be loyal to me! They treat all of us like we don't matter. The only thing they care about is making money—and that goes double for the people I work for!"

That's probably right. Too many companies operate that way now. Even some of the ones that should know better. (See the final chapter on samurai companies.) But too bad! As long as you are paid to work there, you've got to be loyal to the company. If you don't like it, don't work there. As long as you are there, being paid to be there, the duty of loyalty is clear. This is necessary for a variety of reasons, but the most important of which is that a samurai dishonors himself or herself when they act disloyally. **To a samurai, dishonoring oneself is never acceptable!** Never in this case really does mean never. (The honor part of the Samurai Code is all inclusive.)

It is intuitively obvious that acting disloyally is a bad thing. So the question is, to whom is loyalty owed? And since this is about managing, the issue here is loyalty to a company that isn't loyal back. And the answer is—**yes!**

The reason it has to be **YES** is obvious once you answer **NO** to the following questions:

- Is it okay to be disloyal to the individuals that work for you?
- Is it okay to be disloyal to your fellow employees?
- Is it okay to be disloyal to the shareholders in the company?
- Is it okay to be disloyal to the retired employees of the company who are relying on the company's continued success to pay retirement benefits?

If you answered YES to any of the questions above, you can stop reading. This book is not for you. (You might want the phone number of a good lawyer.)

When It's Hard to Be Loyal

"Okay—I got that. But what do I do about management? What if I don't agree with what they are doing? Am I supposed to be loyal to them?"

Good question. And the answer is—it depends. First, just because you disagree with them doesn't mean they are not right. Maybe they are wrong, but they are doing what they think is best for the company. Give them the benefit of the doubt, but share your views. Your duty of loyalty is to the company, not management per se. Of course, it gets harder when you think management is acting unethically, immorally, or criminally. Now your duty to act gets stronger.

"What do you do then?" Obviously, one's actions depend on the circumstances. But here's where a Samurai Leader distinguishes himself or herself. Several elements of the Code come into play.

First, the duty of loyalty to the company requires the samurai manager to address the issue and try to fix it.

Second, his or her sense of rectitude and determination to act wisely encourages him or her to consult with others and to view the matter free of self-interest.

Lastly, after concluding what is the right thing to do, the Samurai Leader has the courage to take the necessary action.

The elements of the Code are meant to be mutually supportive in this manner. Loyalty without rectitude and courage is relatively meaningless. The Code acts as a symbiotic whole.

It should also be noted here that a million years of evolution favors the concept of loyalty. Man is tribal by nature. Confronted by the ice ages, by woolly mammoths and saber-toothed tigers, man could not survive on his own. Expulsion from the tribe meant death. The lone wolf metaphor has a superficial attraction, but really doesn't work for most people. In the modern world, the tribe to which most people are most connected is the "tribe" of people they work with. Loyalty to the tribe was critical for the first million years and things really haven't changed that much. It's in our DNA. If you betray your tribe, it's not going to make you happy. If you let the tribe down by not taking the right action when you should, it's not going to make you happy.

QUESTIONS TO CONSIDER

1. Are you loyal to anyone or anything no matter what? Where do you draw the line?

2. Do you want or expect people to be loyal to you no matter what? Where should they draw the line?

Moving Forward

All right! You are halfway through the Samurai Code as interpreted for business leaders. Honor, courage, rectitude, and loyalty have all been presented and you are beginning to see how they are interconnected. Moreover, you are starting to realize that this samurai thing could be for real in this twenty-first century—and a part of you is wishing you had never picked up this book! This could change things for you. HAVE COURAGE AND KEEP READING!

CHAPTER THREE

THE CODE OF THE SAMURAI
PART II:
COMPASSION, HONESTY, POLITENESS AND SELF-CONTROL

Compassion, Benevolence, Appreciation of the Arts

Bushi no Nasake means *the tenderness of a warrior.* It expresses the ideal of balance for a samurai: a man of war with a caring heart and an understanding of beauty. This fusion of martial valor with cultivation of the arts and compassion for others distinguishes samurai from the hard-edged warriors of other cultures. Their determined acceptance of death heightened their reverence for the beautiful moments of life. Nor did they see one's sense of beauty and compassion as separate things, but rather that one bloomed naturally out of the other, each synergistically flowing from their combination.

This symbiosis of life and death is highlighted in two scenes from the movie *The Last Samurai.* During the middle of the movie, the heroic samurai leader pauses in front of a cherry blossom tree in full glory to say to the Tom Cruise character, a man haunted by his past, "A man could spend his entire life just looking for the perfect blossom and it wouldn't be a wasted life." Then at the end of the movie, as the samurai leader lie dying after a brutal battle, his mind fights past the blood and the pain to a final vision of cherry blossoms and his final enigmatic words are, "They are all perfect."

Yamamoto Tsunetomo, the seventeenth-century samurai whose work *Hagakure* captures so well the essence of a samurai, wrote:

What is called generosity is really compassion. In the Shin'ei it is written "Seen from the eye of compassion, there is no one to be disliked. One who has sinned is to be pitied all the more." There is no limit to the breadth and depth of one's heart. There is room enough for all. That we still worship the sages of the three ancient kingdoms is because their compassion reaches us today.

Whatever you do should be done for the sake of your master and parents, the people in general, and for posterity. The wisdom and courage that come from compassion are real wisdom and courage. When one pun- ishes or strives with the heart of compassion, what he does will be limitless in strength and correctness. Doing something for one's own sake is shallow and mean and turns into evil.[6]

The Compassionate Leader

"Wait a minute! What does this have to do with being a better manager? What do hearts and flowers have to do with that?"

It's about balance. Yin and yang. The best leaders are never one dimensional. Nor are they bad guys. Who wants to follow a bad guy? Real leaders genuinely care for their people. If you want your employees to care enough for you that they will go that extra mile, you have to care for them. You have to do it first. And you can't just tell them that you care, you have to show it and you have to mean it.

Take the idea of "charisma." You want to be a charismatic leader, don't you? Some people have it. Some do not. Do you have to be born with it—or can you learn it?

Interestingly, it seems to come in all shapes and sizes. John F. Kennedy had it. So did Martin Luther King Jr. Unfortunately, so did Adolph Hitler and Mussolini. Bill Clinton has it. Most business executives don't seem to have it, but a few do. Is there a common characteristic of those that have it?

The answer is **yes.**

The secret to charisma is the ability to communicate a vision that will be good for each of that leader's followers, followers who each know that that leader **cares for them!**

Guess how much charisma a manager has who pulls his team together and tells them that he wants to buy a Mercedes so he needs them to really work hard and drive sales like they've never driven them before. Does the word "zero" come to mind?

The point here is that leadership without compassion is fruitless. It loses its power. It ultimately doesn't take anyone anywhere—who wants to follow such a person?

A SAMARAI LEADER STORY

Fern, a blonde-haired, blue-eyed homecoming queen from the small town of Miami, Oklahoma, found an opportunity after college to travel abroad by volunteering at children's hospitals in Russia and South Africa. She was horrified upon meeting victims of the Chernobyl nuclear disaster in Russia and stunned by the prospects of the South African children where so little equality existed.

She returned to the United States and earned her law degree, determined to use it to help make a positive contribution to people. As a young lawyer in Tulsa, she earned a reputation as being innovative, creative, and a tireless worker. Fellow lawyers admired her and knew she would go far.

She did go far—saying goodbye to a lucrative legal career, she joined the Peace Corps. In 2000, she went to Namibia and opened a legal clinic that focused on women's rights. Later she went to Guinea to investigate claims of sexual abuse of female refugees there.

In 2003, Fern agreed to go to Iraq to work for women's rights. Warned by many of the danger, she resolved to go anyway. Showing the same relentless determination to help make a difference, she fought the established male dominance to increase the rights of women there. She had her victories. She stood out as someone who really could change the traditional role that women could play in Iraqi society. That made her a target.

On March 9, 2004, five gunmen armed with AK-47s opened fire in a planned ambush of Fern and two of her colleagues, killing all of them.

In Iraq, in an honor normally reserved for heads of state, three days of mourning were declared as a memorial to Fern. At home, the governor of her home state bestowed on her the Heroic Oklahoman award.

Fern's bravery and her sense of compassion were inextricably combined. Like a nurse or a doctor dealing with a deadly epidemic, a sense of duty and compassion gave her the courage to risk her life for others. Courage and compassion are symbiotic, each nourishing the other.

Too many business leaders do not understand the power of compassion. They believe that because there is no entry in the financial statements for compassion that it therefore does not show up on the bottom line. Yet in their daily lives the power of compassion is recognized—it is a cornerstone of every major religion. (It is another example of how we treat our personal lives and our business lives as if they were two different lives!) Yet, even as they balk at the idea of being compassionate in business, they talk about "caring for their employees" and "caring for the customer"!

Leadership with compassion is far more enduring and growth oriented than leadership through fear. And it doesn't necessarily cost any more! This isn't about raising employee benefits or increasing severance pay for terminated employees. This isn't about not holding employees to high standards. It is about wanting what is best for your employees and customers—it is about caring what happens to them. When employees and customers know you truly care about them, they will trust you and stay with you oftentimes when the dollar and cents issues tell them they shouldn't.

The Artful Leader

"OK—I get it. Compassion—caring for others—it makes sense that a good manager really needs to care about his people. They'll perform a lot better. Although, I've got to tell you that I had a boss once who scared the hell out of everybody and boy did we jump to do whatever he wanted! But why did samurai make a big deal about flowers and poetry? And do I have to get into nature and literature or music, you know, artsy stuff?"

You're probably getting tired of hearing this: **Everything is connected, everything is inter-related.**

The more one pauses to consider the natural world and cultivates one's sense of art, the more one connects to the beauty of the world as it is. One can marvel at a stunning sunset or at the magnificence of a giant sequoia and take strength from being a part of it all. A person is not naturally isolated from his environment—to the extent we distance ourselves from it, we become smaller and greyer, less vibrant. We become less than what we are and we are weaker for it. Our spirit shrinks. Our joy diminishes. We become greater victims to stress and strain. We become worse leaders.

Similarly, artistry arises out of sensitivity. The greater the art, the more powerful the connection to the pain, joy, passion, or cool intelligence of the artist's vision. The greater the art and the vision, the greater everyone's sense of shared experience—and that leads back to compassion for others. Our experiences are not unique, our existence is not meant to be solo.

- "No man is an island unto himself, but each a part of the continent." (John Dunne—not a samurai, but someone who obviously "got it.")
- "To believe that what is true for you in your private heart is true for all men—that is genius." (Ralph Waldo Emerson)

"And all this—the appreciation of art, compassion for others—is going to make me a better manager? A Samurai leader? I don't see how that connects! I thought this book was about being a warrior."

This is another example of the Zen influence on samurai. Life requires quiet contemplation as well as furious action. Too much of either would become counterproductive. Samurai understood that power came from balance. Victory in a swordfight required the swordsman to be smooth and fluid, even rhythmic. Losing one's balance could be death. This same awareness was brought to their life as a whole.

It is no different for a Samurai Leader. Sorry to say, playing hard is not the antidote to working hard. In the daily barrage of meetings, sales quotas, personnel issues, management conflicts, and competitive threats, a manager's warrior spirit will be worn down. Without countervailing, enriching, and calming experiences, the manager's sense of balance will be lost and critical mistakes will be made. Smart managers who lose their balance, who lose touch with other people, who find no respite in the beauty of a cherry blossom, make dumb mistakes! They lose all enjoyment. They hate their jobs. They want a new life.

"All right! I got it! But that doesn't mean I can do it. I'm too stressed. I don't have the time! And I don't know how—I really don't know how."

Relax! Right now we're focused on what the Code is and why it is. And we are not quite done. There's still more of the Code to know. After this chapter, we'll get to how to do it. It's not as hard as you think!

QUESTIONS TO CONSIDER

1. When business leaders talk about "caring for employees" or "caring for customers," what do you think they mean? Do they think they mean it when they say it? Do their employees and customers think they mean it?

2. Can seeing a beautiful sunset really make you stronger?

Honesty

A SAMURAI STORY

A VERY SHORT SAMURAI STORY
Because of some business, Morooka Hikoemon was called upon to swear before the gods concerning the truth of a certain matter. But he said, "A samurai's word is harder than metal. Since I have impressed this fact upon myself,

what more can the gods and Buddhas do?"
And the swearing in was cancelled. [7]

Honesty and honor go hand in hand. A samurai's understanding of honesty is no different from our own. There is no need to define it here. The point is, to a samurai, to be dishonest was shameful. It was cowardly.

Similarly, samurai's honor prevented cheating, stealing, and other forms of deceit. So for a Samurai Leader, the rule here is simple: don't be dishonest, don't tell lies, and don't cheat.

A SAMURAI LEADER STORY

A while ago, Bob was head of finance of a middle-sized technology company with several hundred million in revenues. A subsidiary of a much larger holding company, it provided a very sophisticated transaction processing service to a number of very large companies. One day one of his managers came to him and said they had a big problem. The manager had just discovered that because of a programming error, they had been overcharging certain customers over the

THE SAMURAI LEADER

last eighteen months. The total of the over-charges was about $10 million. Bob asked who knew about the problem. He was told only the manager and the programmer knew, and he had been sworn to silence.

Knowing the company did not have the $10 million to pay back, Bob went first to the CEO of the company to determine what should be done. Bob proposed admitting the error to the customers and working out a repayment plan. He thought their customers would go along with that. The CEO rejected that course of action and insisted on taking the problem to his boss, the CEO of the holding company.

The CEO of the holding company, once made aware of the facts, decided to do nothing. He wanted to wait and see if any customer caught the mistake. He didn't want to pay the money back if he didn't have to. The algorithm that determined the amounts billed was very complicated and difficult to audit. Bob argued that they should admit the overcharge and pay it. He was overruled. He considered disclosing the overcharge anyway but he knew that would go badly. Then he had an idea.

He called in the manager and the program-mer. He told the programmer to write a new program that would undercharge those same customers an amount equal to the overcharge over the next eighteen months. He vowed them to total silence—no one from that point on should say a word to anyone. They agreed. Then Bob waited, knowing that it probably would get out, but he had done what he could.

The secret was kept and no one ever discovered what really happened. Eighteen months later, Bob had the program corrected. As it turned out, Bob became CEO of the tech company. Somehow, it was just understood after he took over that business there would always be done ethically—that you always treated your customers well, no matter what.

A Different Form of Honesty

This Samurai Leader story illustrates an important lesson. One could argue that Bob should have gone public with the overcharge as soon as it was clear that his company did not intend to recognize it. That approach would at first glance seem the most courageous and honest. However, to do so would have hurt more people than it helped. The overcharged customers probably would not have been paid any earlier because the company did not have that much available cash. A settlement like what actually occurred would have been likely. Also, the company's reputation would have been irreparably harmed for what was an honest mistake in the program. Additionally, Bob would have hurt both his own career and those of others. His solution solved the problem in a reasonable way, mindful of all the likely consequences.

There is a different form of honesty that is too often ignored in business. It does not involve right or wrong from a moral viewpoint. Rather, it is about managing to the facts of situations. It requires intellectual honesty. In most challenging business environments there are unpleasant and often threatening facts and circumstances that are more easily ignored than squarely faced.

They come in many shapes and sizes, but they are never fun to deal with. They can be about friends who are not competent, problems for which there are no apparent politically acceptable solutions, competitors that really are better, or issues that are ugly and thorny that maybe will simply go away on their own. These types of situations require intellectual honesty. They must be seen for what they are. Without a rigorous viewpoint, the underlying problems are never solved. Invariably they grow larger and ultimately undermine otherwise potentially successful endeavors.

Samurai Leaders see things the way they really are —they practice intellectual honesty!

Sword

Strokes

TACKLING HUGE GOALS

Good leaders believe that they and their teams can accomplish Herculean tasks. They are not afraid of going after the BHAGs (Big, Hairy, Audacious Goals). To excite, embolden, and exhort their teams, the leaders will emphasize the team's strengths and capabilities, the timeliness of the opportunity, and the justness of their victory. The leader's own conviction must seem almost boundlessly positive. They make success seem almost predestined. They infuse their belief into the hearts and minds of their followers.

But there is a trap! Invariably those BHAGs are difficult for very good reasons. The big business success stories are never slam dunks! The competition will fight back, product development will screw up, trees will obscure the view of the forest, and it will be much harder than it seems it should be. So, a strong leader must be able to accomplish a strange psychological bifurcation.

The leader must portray great confidence in being able to accomplish the BHAG while at the same time always being aware of all the barriers that will get in the way. They will have to listen to all the problems patiently and mindfully. In their own excitement, they can't wish the problems away—even though they really don't want to hear why someone thinks it can't be done.

Samurai Leaders can't ever let problems get the best of them.

QUESTIONS TO CONSIDER

1. When you run a meeting, do you push everyone to the truth of things?

2. Are you honest with yourself when dealing with others?

Politeness, Good Manners

Samurai believed in an elaborate social etiquette as a ritualized structure for daily interaction with the society at large. Detailed guidelines existed for everything from bowing and dining to walking and standing around. Good manners were more than just evidence of good breeding and proper education. They were deemed a demonstration of a samurai's character. Politeness was understood to be an outgrowth of sympathy and compassion for others, but it also was used to demonstrate gracefulness and complete composure.

One who exhibited bad manners was deemed lacking in self-control and awareness of others. In challenging circumstances, grace and politeness were also proofs of reservoirs of strength. When faced with battle, a samurai's politeness and composure were clear evidence of his fearlessness.

Politeness and compassion are obviously closely linked. It is bad manners to tread on the feelings of others. Politeness, by setting rules of conduct, makes coexisting among a warrior class far less abrasive. Everyone's sensitivities are accounted for. Distinctions between class are addressed and the appropriate form of respect can be paid. Strict rules of politeness make a lot of sense when everyone is walking around carrying swords!

Politeness in Business

The requirement of politeness for a Samurai Leader may be less obvious. So many managers treat subordinates rudely that it seems to be a privilege of promotion—the higher one is in an organization, the more employees one can abuse through insensitivity, brutish behavior, and egotistical posturing. Needless to say, such behavior is counterproductive in any workplace where the functioning of a team is important. In today's business conditions, that is just about everywhere.

Politeness is an important tool for a manager—and an undervalued one. Corporations by virtue of their fluid and often complex hierarchical structure create a myriad of daily social interactions. A manager whose behavior is always composed, respectful of everyone, and observant of the etiquette of an office place is someone whom everyone will be happy to work with. In an environment increasingly focused on building teams, this becomes an important attribute.

Of all the samurai behaviors, politeness is the easiest to adopt—and it pays off immediately! The reason it works so quickly is that when you are polite to others, you are inherently granting them respect! And people love being respected. (And frankly, you can fake it if you want to. It still works!) When you are polite, you don't interrupt conversations, you hold doors, you say good morning, you express sympathy when people are hurting. This is easy! People notice this stuff! And they will appreciate you for doing it. Being respectful of others is HUGE and politeness is such a simple way to show it.

Politeness—another part of the Code for a Samurai Leader.

QUESTIONS TO CONSIDER

1. What little things can you do at the office to show you respect those who work near you?

2. Compare someone you know who is very impolite with someone you know who is very polite. Is there a big difference in how others treat them?

Self-Control

A samurai was expected to display a certain stoicism. Displaying reaction to discomfort, complaining of excessive heat or cold, or moaning about the conditions of life were antithetical to the Way of the samurai. Emotions generally were not to be shown in public. Ideally, a samurai would display no sign of joy or anger, nor dwell on any personal grief—although it was an appropriate measure of "the tenderness of a warrior" to share the grief of another.

For a samurai, however, self-control went well beyond mere stoicism. It was the hardened frame on which the whole of his character was maintained. The Samurai Code exerted a constant discipline that required an extreme diligence. A person whose passions were not kept in check would soon fail to meet the standards set for samurai.

To again quote Yamamoto Tsunetomo:

At a glance, every individual's own measure of dignity is manifested just as it is. There is dignity in personal appearance. There is dignity in a calm aspect. There is dignity in a paucity of words. There is dignity in flawlessness of manners. There is dignity in solemn behavior. And there is dignity in deep insight and a clear perspective.

These are all reflected on the surface. But in the end, their foundation is simplicity of thought and tautness of spirit.[8]

"Tautness of spirit"—that doesn't cut much slack!

The Self-Controlled Leader

Self-control in business is no less critical. If one can't control oneself, how can one control others? In anyone's career there come times when big deals come down to final minutes or major decisions can be postponed no longer—when stresses and strains flame up at a particular moment in time. To demonstrate a calm exterior amidst those moments of panic and pandemonium, when everyone else is overreacting and under-achieving—in those moments, reputations are made.

Passion and enthusiasm in business are wonderful assets in leaders; however, uncontrolled they quickly turn into liabilities, untrusted and unmanageable. Anger is particularly double-edged. There are times when a manager needs to be angry to be most effective, when his team really isn't performing and needs a psychic kick. But even then, the manager needs to be in complete self-control, wielding his or her anger like a scalpel and limiting the cuts to a very specific purpose. Those instances when a display of anger is the best course of action are exceedingly rare, and those managers emotionally equipped to use it effectively are uncommon. Usually there are better ways to deal with the situation. Anger is not a privilege of management—its effects are too destructive.

Athletes learn that to perform their best they need "to stay within themselves." The mind must be quieted and awareness must be centered on the task. Tiger Woods in the final round of the Masters golf tournament, Joe Montana on a game-winning touchdown drive, Serena Williams serving out a match at the US Open—all are in complete self-control. The demands on a manager to work at his or her best are no less, though the stakes may be very different. A Samurai Leader is always under control, composed, and clear minded.

The discipline to be in complete control when it matters most is not something that arises naturally. It takes work! It's a way of approaching every day with a sense of purpose, with an understanding of what can be accomplished at what risks. It's a way of facing the risks without fear. Fear is the ultimate thief of self-control.

Sword

Strokes

CAREER MISTAKES

Most career-limiting actions are self-inflicted! In business, there are countless ways to screw up and new ways are always being invented. But invariably when a manager screws up, he should have known better *and usually did know better!* Every one knows: be careful what you say about the boss, don't party 'til all hours before big meetings, the office is not a singles bar, get your work done on time, etc. The list is endless!

Business is much less anonymous than it seems to be at first. A manager's career is often within just one industry—even if within several different companies. Within the largest industries, the degree of separation is still small. Especially as one climbs the corporate ladder, everyone is known by somebody—and usually a lot of somebodies. It's very hard to bury one's past. One's reputation travels everywhere and quickly.

Self-discipline is enormously important for a manager. A lot of management involves dealing with temptations that are put in your path. Other people's money may come through your hands, inappropriate solicitations may be made to you, and inequalities in power create opportunities for abuse.

Whenever you find yourself losing your self-control, or are confronted by things you are not ready to deal with, get away to somewhere you can be alone QUICK! Talk to someone you trust to determine the best course of action. Find a way to not do or say things that will come back to hurt you.

Remember, you are the only one who is likely to ruin your career!

The higher one rises in an organization, the more one must demonstrate self-control. All of a leader's actions take place under a magnifying glass. A sarcastic joke can be perceived as a biting criticism. A fleeting glance of concern can send tremors rippling through a department. Impatience resulting from a headache can be taken personally by all you encounter. People derive so many clues as to what's "really" going on from mere appearances of things that a leader who does not exercise self-control will constantly be communicating unintended "realities." Spontaneity can be a great thing in a leader, but that leader better really know what he or she is doing with it!

QUESTIONS TO CONSIDER

1. How often do you say or do things that you are sorry about afterwards?

2. Do you hold yourself to high standards?

Bringing It All Together

It is undeniable that acting like a samurai in business is no easy thing to do. It's not showing you the "one thing" you've got to do to succeed, the seven habits you have to have, or the specific rules you have to follow. In fact, if you've been paying attention, you know that acting samurai is not something you'll be able to do just at work. It will infiltrate everything. You've also figured out that it all ties together, so it really isn't something that you pick and choose. *And that's the point!* Every action one takes is just another link in the chain of causation that makes up a life. We are what we do. Of course, it all comes together. Do you really believe that you can separate your actions so that one does not lead to the next?

Here is how the Code of the Samurai all comes together:

The Code of the Samurai Leader

- **Act honorably.** Honor isn't negotiable. It is an overarching requirement.
- **Act with courage and a warrior's spirit.** When you know what needs to be done, do it.
- **Act with rectitude.** Do the right thing.
- **Be loyal.** Without loyalty, there is no trust.
- **Be compassionate.** To be a leader one must care for others.
- **Appreciate the arts.** Art is a doorway to understanding and appreciating life.
- **Be honest.** Without honesty, there is no credibility.
- **Be polite.** It shows respect and makes getting along with everyone much easier.
- **Act under self-control.** To manage others one must manage oneself.

That's it! That's the Code of the Samurai and the Code of the Samurai Leader.

You can stop reading now if all you wanted was to know what you had to do to be a Samurai Leader. Or you can read more books on samurai and extrapolate for yourself what lessons should be learned for today's world. Then you can act on that.

Or not. The challenge, of course, is in the doing. To be a Samurai Leader you have to do all of it, all the time. It works because it is interdependent. Each element that is lived by makes the other elements easier to accomplish. Read further and what you'll get is a path to the Way of the Leader—a path to a way of being that turns courage into fearlessness, intelligence into wisdom, and satisfaction into joy. For those were the true goals of a samurai. Right actions flow naturally out of the right way of being.

This pathway will not require years of psychoanalysis, pain and suffering, or religious conversion. It will require a change in the way you perceive your surroundings (focused on the business world of the Samurai Leader). A different philosophical viewpoint will be presented—but it won't hurt! And everything that follows will make you a better manager and a happier one—a fearless one! I promise!

CHAPTER FOUR

THE WARRIOR MANAGER

To succeed in business a leader must win most of the battles he or she fights. He doesn't have to win them all, but if he doesn't win most of the time—and particularly win the battles that count the most—he won't succeed. Some battles can be avoided, many can't. They come in all shapes and sizes, and the opposition can be individuals, ideas, prior experiences, or cultural tendencies. A manager is going to have to lead his team through, over, and past a myriad of obstacles. Knowing what battles to fight is important. Knowing when and who (or what) to fight is important. Knowing how to fight is important. But most important is knowing you have to fight.

Prepared to Fight

Samurai Leaders fight. They fight in order to get the right things done, they fight fearlessly, they fight mindfully. They fight with honor and compassion. They are warriors.

Being warriors and knowing they have to fight, they are always prepared for battle. That alone will distinguish them from most managers. Most managers are not prepared to fight. And when confronted by a fight, most managers don't want to be in the front lines and certainly don't want to lead the charge. That's why over time Samurai Leaders will always get their chance to demonstrate their abilities.

A great example of this was the rise of Ulysses S. Grant during the Civil War. He was not at all noteworthy at the beginning of the war, but by the end of it he was in command of the Union army. He did what President Lincoln most needed him to do: he fought battles. Before Grant took command, Lincoln was frustrated by generals who loved being at the head of the army but were reluctant to fight. But Grant, remorselessly, brutally, and with infinite determination, bulldozed the rebel army with his superior resources.

Since this is about business and not wars, the morality issues are different, as are tactics and strategies. The warrior's skills need to be different. Also, because it is business, it is a lifetime of battles with shifting alliances, shifting resources, and shifting goals and objectives. Because so much will change during a Samurai Leader's career, he or she must learn and be prepared to fight in whatever manner will be most effective, given the circumstances.

The battles to be fought vary dramatically. Some will be internal fights and some will be external, both can leave blood on the floor. Some battles will be obvious, many won't be. Sometimes one only learns of a battle after it has been lost.

Identify Battles Early

The first requirement in winning battles is identifying them as early as possible! Most of the external battles are pretty obvious. There will be battles over market share, winning lawsuits, obtaining financing at optimum rates, signing big deals, negotiating supplier agreements, mergers and acquisitions, and opening new markets, to name just a few. Less obvious are the battles over product development—new competitive offerings may be under development that a competing company doesn't even know about. Also new competitors may be planning to come into a market with huge resources and a hunger for expansion.

In contrast, most of the internal battles are not obvious. Yet, they can be the most brutal and the most devastating. The political battles over management and leadership positions are frequently relatively invisible and often involve factors unknown to those most concerned. Battles over organizational restructuring are constant and the power players often deceptively manipulative. There will be battles over responsibility for successes and for failures, sometimes with individuals claiming credit where they had no actual involvement or placing blame where no blame is due.

The important point here is that a Samurai Leader, knowing that battles are inevitable, is constantly on the lookout for them. "Forewarned is forearmed." The earlier a battle is identified, the better the preparation, the stronger the fortification. Alliances can be negotiated and potential enemies can be neutralized.

Preparing for Battle

"But there are so many battles!"

Exactly. There's no way to identify here all the different battles that will need to be fought. Similarly, there is no single set of strategies or tactics that will guarantee victories. There are too many variables. This was true in samurai times just as it is today. Nonetheless, with five hundred years of warfare to draw on, samurai found certain ways of being to be useful—certain ways of preparing oneself and certain ways of responding to threats.

One of the best-known texts is *The Book of Five Rings* by Miyamoto Musashi written in 1643.

Famous as a superb and deadly swordsman, Musashi's work is both a how-to manual on fighting with a sword as well as a manual on the art of war. It is pragmatic and tactical in nature, with an emphasis on maintaining an awareness during battle so as to avoid predictability and constraining limitations. In one passage, he summarizes the approach necessary for continuing success:

For people who want to learn my military science, there are rules for learning the art:

1. *Think of what is right and true.*
2. *Practice and cultivate the science.* (Then: Training with weapons. Now: Know the tools of management science, understand business process methodologies and analytics.)
3. *Become acquainted with the arts.* (This advice goes to both increasing one's cultural awareness as well as understanding that the "art" in the art of war and in martial arts requires an awareness of psychological and environmental factors.)
4. *Know the principles of the crafts.* (Then: How to make a sword. Now: Accounting, Legal, Marketing.)
5. *Understand the harm and benefit in everything.* (Risk and reward.)
6. *Learn to see everything accurately.* (Think objectively.)

7. *Become aware of what is not obvious.* (See what others don't see.)
8. *Be careful even in small matters.*
9. *Do not do anything useless.* (Don't do things that are wastes of time.)

Winning through Management

Musashi recognized that winning battles acting solely as an individual will only take one so far. A leader must act on a broader scale. To do so, the leader must adapt to the requirements imposed by those he would lead.

Musashi goes on to add:

> Also, large-scale military science is a matter of winning at keeping good people, winning at employing large numbers of people, winning at correctness of personal conduct, winning at governing nations, winning at taking care of the populace, winning at carrying out customary social observances. In whatever field of endeavor, knowledge of how to avoid losing out to others, how to help oneself, and how to enhance one's honor, is part of military science.[9]

What this means for the Samurai Leader is that to succeed over the whole of one's career, the manager must see both the depth and the breadth of the stage on which he or she is acting. A narrow view of things ultimately fails. Small issues can lead to large defeats. Victory comes to the one who is best prepared, understands the most, and who then strikes and fights without doubts or fears. A samurai's action flows from a comprehensive awareness and a disciplined and balanced mind channeled by training and an aggressive spirit. The ideals of the samurai, perhaps more than any other class of warriors, emphasize the mindfulness necessary for success in battle.

Remaining Calm

This point is beautifully made in another famous samurai text written by a renowned warrior and successful leader in 1632. In *The Book of Family Traditions on the Art of War*, Yagyu Munenori writes about the necessary balance between thought and action. Although he is writing specifically about how to win a sword fight, his words are intended to be broadly applicable.

> *The point is to be calm and quiet above while sustaining an aggressive mood underneath...of being extremely serene, unruffled, and calm on the surface, while inwardly being aggressively watchful.*
>
> *It is bad when the body, hands, and feet are hurried. The aggressive and passive modes should be paired, one inward and one outward;*

it is bad to settle into just one mode. It is imperative to reflect on the sense of yin and yang alternating. Movement is yang, stillness is yin. Yin and yang interchange, inside and outside. When yang moves inwardly, outwardly be still, in the yin mode; when you are inwardly yin, movement appears outwardly. In this kind of martial art as well, inwardly you activate your mental energy, constantly attentive, while outwardly you remain unruffled and calm. This is yang moving within, while yin is quiet without. This is in accord with the pattern of nature.

Furthermore, when outwardly intensely aggressive, if you are calm within while aggressive without, so that your inner mind is not captured by the outside, then you will not be outwardly wild. If you move both inwardly and outwardly at once, you become wild. The aggressive and passive modes, movement and stillness, should be made to alternate inside and outside.[10]

In the daily strife of modern business, perhaps no lesson could be more useful than this passage quoted from an early seventeenth-century samurai who was the trusted advisor to the shogun. As Munenori stresses, when in the midst of heated action, remain cool and calm. When a deal starts going south, when your boss starts yelling and screaming, when deadlines are moments away and immediate action is required, when the buzz all around is frantic and chaotic (we've all been there!), that is when one's mind must remain calm, unruffled, and clear. When one's actions must be quick and decisive, one's mind must be focused and serene.

Similarly, when in the midst of a business battle and when your mind is reacting aggressively to threats and challenges, when it is screaming for violent action, let there be no outward show of it. Display only the customary at-ease demeanor. An aggressive mind coupled with aggressive actions produces wild behavior, which is rarely productive in the long run. Battles are not won that way!

"Sure, that sounds great. But how do you actually do it? When the emotions start getting hot, how are you supposed to keep everything under control?"

The first requirement to maintaining control is to understand and accept the need for doing so. A samurai understands that there is never a time when it is acceptable to lose self-control. Never! Especially not during a battle. Someone who cannot control himself has no chance of controlling the surrounding situation or other people who are involved.

Maintaining self-control is a matter of discipline. Whether the matter is large or small, one's approach should be the same. By practicing self-control all the time, it will be there when it is most needed. But self-control is not just a matter of burying emotions under layers of external calm. That approach turns an individual into a volcano soon to erupt. **True self-control comes from morphing together mindfulness and fearlessness.**

More than anything, this book is about how to attain these two states of being. They are attainable by everyone to various degrees. They are important in every facet of one's life, but are particularly valuable when facing challenges. They are essential attributes in a leader—and the higher you rise, the more important they become. When dealing with battles they can be the difference between winning and losing. Leaders who are afraid transmit fear to their followers and leaders who are not wise are not worth following. Below is just an introductory chart; the next several chapters go into much more detail.

MINDFULNESS	FEARLESSNESS
➤ Think of doing the right thing	➤ Do the right thing
➤ Train the mind	➤ Training • Skills • Fitness
➤ Think aggressively	➤ Think positively
➤ Think objectively	➤ Confront your fears
➤ Think without attachment	➤ Non-Attachment to consequences • No clinging, be cool

The parallel nature of the factors that produce mindfulness and fearlessness are not coincidental. First, they are irrevocably bound together through their common heritage in Zen philosophy. The way to both fearlessness and mindfulness takes the same path. Moreover, we know they are linked just based on our own common experiences. It is impossible to do one's best thinking when afraid. It is hard to be fearless when one is not confident that one's mind perceives all possibilities and fully understands what is going on. The combination of the two, however, is powerful. It is also intimidating to anyone who comes up against someone who is truly mindful and truly fearless.

Choosing the Battles

A Samurai Leader acting with mindfulness and fear-lessness will be prepared to fight and win battles over the course of a career. However, that does not mean that he should fight every battle or that he will always win. A Samurai Leader still needs to determine which battles should be fought and which should be avoided.

People who fight battles that they don't belong in too often lose the battles that do matter to them. The Samurai Code was developed to help samurai decide when they should draw their swords and when they should keep them sheathed.

If, based on the circumstances, one must fight in order to act in accordance with the Code, then one should fight. If acting in accordance with the Code requires peace, then one should not take up the sword.

Similarly, a Samurai Leader should look to the Code to determine actions to be taken. However, the Code is not intended to determine tactics and strategies appropriate to achieving a certain individual's goals and objectives. Other criteria are necessary to make those determinations.

A warrior spirit can get a reckless and undisciplined Samurai Leader in a lot of trouble. Unless no alternative is available, battles should be avoided unless they meet the following three requirements:

1. The Samurai Leader is passionate about the issue,
2. The Samurai Leader is sure of his ability to win the battle, and
3. The benefits of winning the battle are consistent with the Samurai Leader's goals and objectives and have a solid ROI (return on investment for the resources used in fighting the battle).

PASSION

Don't participate in battles that you don't really care about. It is very easy to get swept up into other peoples' battles and to take sides when it is not really necessary. Only fight battles where you are passionate about the outcome. This is true for both large and small ones. Athletes know that they often get injured when they are not fully committed to the athletic endeavor. Their concentration isn't the same and they get casual about what they are doing and get hurt as a result. Also, coaches rest their top players in meaningless games that don't affect getting to the championship. Samurai Leaders need to approach battles the same way. Unless the outcome really matters to you, don't fight!

WINNING

If you aren't sure you can win, don't fight if you don't have to. Put aside bravado and ego. Analyzing what it takes to win must be done objectively with a rigorous confrontation of the facts and realities. Be sure!

Also, make sure that you have more firepower than you need. Battles rarely go as planned and there are usually more obstacles than first anticipated. Opponents will often never begin the fight if they see that you are going to win regardless of how well they fight. Also, in maintaining allies, it is important that they see that winning is assured. If they start seeing that losing is a real possibility, they are far more likely to disappear when they are needed.

R O I

Whether it is corporate politics or a battle over an acquisition or a fight for market share, only fight when the benefits of victory 1) support attaining the core goals and objectives, and 2) are worth the economic, social, and political costs of fighting the battle. Without the discipline of adhering to both requirements, one can waste important resources that may not later be available for much more essential issues.

Of the two requirements, it is more often the first one that isn't examined closely. Managers see an area of opportunity that offers an exciting economic return and go after it even though it is not consistent with stated goals or objectives. But it is exciting to enter the battle for it and soon the resources are tied up fighting for it when they should be used elsewhere. With this approach, managers end up winning battles and losing wars.

But the second requirement of assessing the true economic, social, and political costs of staging a battle also needs a highly disciplined analysis. Battles invariably cost more in time and energy than anticipated and rarely go as planned. Whether the manager is waging the battle for himself or for the unit or entity he is managing, battles tax emotional and economic resources that are not easily replaced.

Lastly, a highly structured and rigorous analysis of the benefits of victory must be done. Too often the fight becomes brutal and the rewards minimal. The surgery was successful, but the patient died. Don't over forecast; don't fall in love with an anticipated outcome.

Battles That Must Be Fought

There is an important corollary to fighting only the right battles. **Never avoid a battle that must be fought.**

Most people don't really want to fight, so it is easy for them to talk themselves out of fighting. Avoiding a battle is especially appealing when the short-term consequences of fighting appear negative—which is often the case. It is easier to just go along with what's happening. The long-term consequences of avoiding necessary battles, however, can be disastrous. Not only are there the immediate effects related to not standing up to the current situation, there is also the significant negative consequence of increasing insecurities.

When one fails to fight when that action is clearly called for, one's sense of self takes a beating. Regardless of excuses or rationales for failing to fight, the real self inside knows better and is diminished. The resulting loss of confidence creates a series of adverse effects: anger, stress, fear, and depression—increased insecurity. Additionally, it makes standing up and fighting in the future that much harder.

Similarly, every battle experienced increases one's awareness of what it takes to win. It also improves one's fighting capabilities. It's like the advantage of having made the playoffs before in professional sports. Experience counts. One learns that the opposition invariably has its own challenges to overcome. The opposing managers are probably not samurai and have their own fears and liabilities. They are not as hard to beat as they seem.

A Samurai Leader thinking objectively can take advantage of the subjective thinking of his opponents. Once one understands the emotional drivers of the opposition, a battle plan can be developed that takes advantage of the blind spots that will exist because of the emotional biases. One manipulates others by giving them what they want. Most of the time, subjectively driven individuals do not want the things that lead to long-term victory; most wants are driven by an emotional attachment and are short-term by nature. So, a Samurai Leader will give away the apple in order to gain the apple tree.

Will and Determination

There is one last factor that must be a part of a Samurai Leader.

"Victory at all costs, victory in spite of all terror, victory however long and hard the road may be; for without victory there is no survival." So said Winston

Churchill during England's dark days at the beginning of World War II. Perhaps no leader is more justly famous than Churchill for the power a single man's will and determination had on a nation as a whole.

History is filled with stories of leaders whose will and determination made the difference between victory and defeat: Lincoln during the Civil War, Washington at Valley Forge, Mao Zedong during the Long March. Similarly, business leaders have fought through staggering challenges and built great companies that would otherwise have collapsed but for their leaders' refusal to quit.

In the recently published bestseller *Good to Great*, Jim Collins's study of companies like Kimberly-Clark, Kroger, Walgreens, Gillette, Wells Fargo, and Fannie Mae revealed certain common characteristics in the success stories of each of these great companies.[11] Not surprisingly, in each case there were leaders who shared a "ferocious resolve, an almost stoic determination to do whatever needs to be done to make the company great."

An unwavering will to succeed where others falter is a distinguishing factor at any level of an organization. Salesmen who refuse to lose a sale, research scientists who go down a hundred false trails before finding the right one, managers who push creative solutions through bureaucratic mazes, all exhibit that crucial will and determination that separates them from their competitors.

The samurai histories are also filled with stories of samurai who refused to quit or back down regardless of the odds. Just living to the strictures of the Samurai Code required an unwavering commitment. That commitment to being samurai became so profound that it created that "tautness of spirit" that rests on an individual's will and determination. As such, it becomes a visible manifestation of his character.

The same must be true for a Samurai Leader. It absolutely will take a strong will to act in accordance with the Samurai Leader Code. The manifestation of that will is part of what will drive the success. Will and determination can be contagious. A manager's relentless drive can inspire others. It can be charismatic and motivate followers to accept that manager as their leader. What is certain is that a lack of will ensures failure. Those who quit when the going gets tough never inspire others—they are managers to be avoided. The perception of strength, matched by the reality, is seductive to others around that person.

A side note here is that to win the promotion battles within an organization, managers must manifest their rightness for that next-level job before they actually have the job. They have to "be" it before they have it. If the managers can't see themselves as having all the necessary qualities and characteristics, how can they expect their bosses to see it in them? The essential "will" in this case is the will to become whatever it takes to succeed at the next level—and the level above that.

In summary, there are leaders who abhor warfare and successful managers who do not believe that business is a series of battles. Their mindset is more of cooperation and collective enhancement. They prefer the image of the peacekeeper to that of the warrior. It is important to note that nothing in this book is contrary to that *except* that leadership ultimately always demands aggressiveness. Leaders need a warrior mindset even if they never wield a sword. Gandhi fought battles and won. Jesus' disciples were warriors for their religion even as they preached forgiveness and compassion. The battles are always out there and someone needs to win them.

- **Be willing to fight**
- **Identify battles as early as possible**
- **Remember the yin and yang of action/calm**
- **Develop mindfulness and fearlessness**
- **Choose your battles carefully**
- **Have will and determination**

QUESTIONS TO CONSIDER ———

1. Can you think of confrontations that you avoided that only made the situation worse later?

2. Do you like the idea of being a warrior but cannot really imagine yourself as being one? Why not?

CHAPTER FIVE

SOME COMMON ZENse

Everything in the following chapters is directly relevant to helping ordinary managers become really terrific leaders. Although it may appear it at times, the material is not presented to convert anyone to Zen. If the reader is interested in Zen, there are much better books than this to read. But certain ideas taken from Zen philosophy can be incredibly useful to managers. They are described here to illuminate the interconnectedness of being and doing, thinking and acting. Did you really think you could become a better leader without changing the way you think?

Most samurai were Zen Buddhists. It gave the samurai an intellectual, moral, and spiritual foundation to support that "tautness of spirit" that made samurai unique. The Code of the Samurai is an obvious product of Zen teachings, just like in the Western world our moral codes are driven by Christianity. But unlike Christianity, Zen is more focused on how to be in this world, right now, than upon a relationship to God. One can easily be a good Christian and still benefit from Zen philosophy. It is designed to increase awareness of one's surroundings. It facilitates understanding interrelationships of all kinds. Though it has important spiritual underpinnings, its primary lessons are centered on attaining a wiser and experientially rich existence today. What it offers a Samurai Leader can be empowering, even stripped of its spiritual dimensions.

Zen Leadership

Zen Buddhism is the leanest of religions; it rejects dogma and doctrine, rejects rules and forms, and rejects ceremony and cathedrals. It can be approached just as a philosophy and, in fact, many of the teachings of the Zen masters seem to ignore many of the things that people think of as being religious. Zennists don't talk about creation, there is no devil, and there is no real worshiping. Buddha is the closest thing to God and it's known he walked on this earth and was a man. Zen does show the way to fearlessness; it does open a path to wisdom. Compassion and morality are preached. The Way is there for everyone. It was perfect for samurai.

For the Samurai Leader, the philosophical underpinnings of Zen can be hugely helpful. No religious conversion is necessary. (And none will be preached here!) The spiritual foundation of Zen, though profound in its implications, can be set aside while focus is brought to the perceptual and intellectual advantages to be derived from Zen. It teaches one how to think more clearly.

"Let me get this right. I have to become a Zen Master in order for me to become a Samurai Leader?"

No, that's not the goal of this book, but it is the direction. This is more like Luke Skywalker's education in *The Empire Strikes Back*. In the middle of the movie, Luke spends time with Yoda (definitely a Zen master) in the midst of a swamp learning how to use the Force. Based on what Luke learns there, he comes closer to becoming a Jedi Knight (think Samurai Leader). What Yoda is teaching Luke is how to clear out the clutter of the mind in order to tap into clarity of vision that allows him to fulfill his potentialities. That's Zen!

One goal here is to show how certain principles of Zen can be utilized by a manager to facilitate and empower him or her to act in accordance with the Samurai Code. But additionally, Zen is presented here to provide a powerful and insightful perspective for a manager to view day-to-day occurrences. In business, a manager must distinguish between what is real and what is a mirage, between illusions of control and real power. By using what Zen offers, the manager fulfills potential. It's what Yoda was trying to teach Luke.

Why Learn Zen?

This chapter presents the basics of Zen in order to prepare the reader for what comes in later chapters. The goals of those chapters are to lead a Samurai Leader to **fearlessness** and **mindfulness**, respectively. What is contained in these chapters is not supported by empirical data or documented studies. But they are backed by two thousand years of intellectual development and their content distills and connects that acquired wisdom to the needs of a business manager. In other words, by learning a little bit about Zen here, a pathway will be opened up to lead a manager to a much more stress-free workplace environment—because fear will have dissipated—and to better decision making because that manager's mind will be freed to think more clearly. These goals are achievable.

Additionally, by practicing some of the principles of Zen, a manager can gain control over emotions—both his own and those of others around him. Calmness in the face of strife, clarity in the midst of confusion, control during moments of chaos—with these attributes, managing those crucial career-determining moments becomes easier.

Certain teachings from Zen philosophy promote these attributes. You don't have to be a Zen master to learn some basic career-enhancing skills that samurai used everyday.

You Can Do It!

"Hold on! I'm no good at that lotus position—my legs won't do it. And I'm not into chanting and stuff. Maybe this isn't for me. Can't I be a samurai without all the Zen?"

Relax. You don't have to do any chanting and you won't have to get in the lotus position. But there are some basics to it that can help you be a better manager pretty quickly. Even better, maybe you'll be one of the ones who get Zen right away. Some people get it very quickly—and some never get it. But the worst that will happen to you by reading further is that it will make you cooler at bars and cocktail parties. Now can I go on?

"Okay, but remember, no chanting!"

What Zen Is

Zen, like the Samurai Code, is deceptively simple to understand. It holds that we are all a part of a benevolent cosmic life force through our unique "True Self." As one awakens to one's True Self, "one senses the being of all beings as one great body, suffused with good will, compassion, joy, and equanimity."[12] One obtains an empathic intimacy with all states of being. It is an unrestricted, eternal True Self, not limited by the impermanency of life or death. When one is the True Self, one is aware of all life, joyful in the midst of it, calm and peaceful, with no fear, no anxiety, no restlessness, no anger.

"Say what?"

Imagine you own a bicycle shop in a small town. It's forty years ago and there is no real competition, no discounters, no Wal-Mart, and the bikes you sell are good quality at a very fair price. All the townspeople know you and trust you and you know and like all of them. Business is good. You love what you do. You love living in your small town, enjoying every day, experiencing the change of seasons, watching the children of the town grow up as they buy bigger bikes from you. As you get older, you know you are living a rich and full life. You are perfectly content.

"Okay. I can imagine that someone could find that life perfect. But it wouldn't last! And nobody gets that in today's crazy world!"

Not true. In Zen, when you have found your True Self, you can be like that bicycle storeowner—even if you're a stockbroker living in New York City.

Zen preaches nonattachment. An individual should be free of needing possessions, free of clinging to relationships, free of fixed ideas and prejudgments, free of desires for things not then had, free of past experiences and future concerns. Everything anyone needs, he already has.

Yet, this is not a passive state, not nihilistic, not a quiet rejection of the vibrancy of life. Far from that, it is instead a complete commitment to "now." It embraces the moment that one is in—it denies the future, denies the past—there is only now. The commitment to NOW is so strong that ideally neither thought nor emotion interferes with the experience of whatever it is that is going on in that moment. If there is a beautiful sunset, a Zen master is not thinking about it being beautiful, he is part of it.

If a Zen manager is teaching an employee how to perform some task, he connects to the information instead of thinking about the process or harboring negative emotions about the employee's learning abilities. He experiences that employee's learning. The Zen self and its actions are completely harmonious. Zen is not about sitting around contemplating; it is in fact about acting without contemplation! It's like a top salesman making his sales pitch—the words just flow without him consciously adding one word to the next. If he thought about each word before he said it, it wouldn't sound as natural and he would sound less believable. To contemplate action is to create a barrier to the action itself. Zen empowers action. This is after all the religion of samurai.

The True Self is inside each of us, obscured by mental and emotional barriers that keep us from ourselves. These barriers are the results of earlier miseducation and traumatic experiences that have created warps and discontinuities in the way we approach issues. Everyone has them, such as a child bitten by a big dog who is, even as an adult, afraid of all dogs, or worse, a young manager too often berated by a mean-spirited overbearing boss who comes to believe he has no managerial talent. As one gets deeper into Zen, those barriers disappear. A Zen master exists in a fluid, timeless, open, and completely unencumbered state of being, subject to no dependencies, free and unattached, clinging to nothing, needing nothing—connected to everything through the True Self.

Now frankly, becoming a Zen master would be a stretch for all of us, but by moving in that direction a manager can triumph—Luke Skywalker destroyed the Death Star long before he became a true Jedi Knight.

A result of being one's True Self is to have perfect insight—a deep and complete wisdom. It is a wisdom for which there is no searching. It is a wordless understanding inseparable from being. The very act of searching for it keeps one from it. Instead, one approaches it on the way to the True Self, coming from the outside in, peeling away the artificial layers of thought, perception, and experience, which cloud the ability to truly understand the objective truths and realities of the world. It leads to an unfiltered awareness, free of misperceptions arising from emotionality, the warping effects of desires, and the fog of preconceptions. The awakening to one's True Self can occur in a single leap, an intuitive flash. It does not require years of study or adherence to any dogma or doctrine—such things can even keep one from it.

"Wait a minute. Are you saying that I can be smarter? That if I do all these Zen things that I will be more intelligent? How real is that?!"

What's real is that you are smarter than you think you are. But you are like someone trying to play golf without ever having had a golf lesson. You have all these bad habits. Even a little instruction can make a big difference.

"So why didn't they teach me this in school?"

Who knows? Probably because the roots of Zen are philosophical, not factual. Western education loves the idea of facts and systems. Zen is not about facts and it is not a system. It won't help you learn accounting or law or how to calculate return on investment. But it can make you a better accountant, lawyer, or business leader by helping you to think more objectively and creatively. You'll learn to look at facts differently (a potential that already exists within you).

And that's the executive summary of Zen.

The History of Zen

Now we'll look at the history of Zen. In the beginning, there was Buddha…Well, actually, no. About 500 BC, a prince of India's warrior class started wondering what life was like outside of the palace. His name was Siddhartha Gautama. So, he started venturing out and discovered the suffering of man. He resolved to learn the reality and the meaning of life and spent six years wandering, mastering religions, and experiencing life. Then one day he sat under a tree determined not to move until he understood the nature of existence. He stayed under the tree all night. At the end of the night, he had become enlightened, and had become Buddha. He had realized the truth of Karma and he understood the connectedness and unity of all things. He understood the nature of suffering and how to move past it.

For the next forty years, he went about teaching the *dharma*—the truths he had learned. Over time—a lot of time—Buddhism spread to China and then throughout Asia. As it spread, it broke into a variety of sects and one of those in China became known as *ch'an.* This sect spread to Japan where it became known as Zen.

The key to understanding Zen (and Buddhism generally) is that Siddhartha Gautama's aim was to end the suffering of man. His enlightenment came with a flash of insight that showed him the sources of suffering and the way to move past it. Suffering flowed from a man's desiring things he didn't have. So, the key to ending the suffering was to end the desire for those things. And the key to ending the desire is to show that everything you need to live a full and complete and happy life you already have.

The principles underlying Zen are essential for the Samurai Leader because too many of them are suffering. The stresses and strains of their careers literally cause illness and death. On an everyday basis, a manager's failure to approach the job with a committed and confident attitude diminishes the joy in everyday experiences and limits relationships to fellow workers, friends, and family. It makes doing your job much more difficult. It is an unhealthy way of being.

Removing Barriers

"Let me get this straight. This Zen stuff is important to being a Samurai Leader because it's going to make me happier? This isn't going to turn into one of those 'Don't worry, be happy' kind of deals, is it? I'm not buying that!"

That's not what this is about! This is more about convincing a person at a beach in 90-degree weather to wear a bathing suit instead of five layers of shirts and sweaters and jackets. We make things much harder than they are. We are conditioned from birth through both intended and unintended acts of others to respond like Pavlov's dogs to certain stimuli. Zen is a pathway to de-conditioning yourself from the brainwashing that is aimed at us every day.

Much of the attempted conditioning (brainwashing) is obvious—the relentless daily barrage of advertising—but effective. To quote the Rolling Stones in one of their most famous hits "Satisfaction":

"When I am watching my TV and a man comes and tells me how white my shirts can be,

"But he can't be a man because he doesn't smoke the same cigarettes as me!"

And we know too that our parents, our schools, our friends, our churches, our politicians, the news, and entertainment media all intentionally try to get us to think and act certain ways. They try to make it emotionally important to us to think like them. And we know too of all the unintended acts and events that influence what we do and think because of the random rewards and punishments of our daily existence—all of which have conditioned us to be what we have become. We avoid everything that we think is like something that has once caused us pain. We seek things that are like things that have brought us pleasure. We try to categorize everything, many times forcing things into categories where they don't belong.

The problem is that so much of that conditioning, both intended and unintended, is NEGATIVE! It is not about freeing your mind to think objectively—it is about thinking "their" way. It is crammed full of biases and prejudices. It is learning too much from too little. We become like the child bitten by the dog who becomes prejudiced against all dogs. The random events and outcomes of our past experiences become the major influencers of our future actions. Your past should not dictate your future!

Zen is about simplifying and clarifying. This is about making better decisions by enabling the manager to see what is real and what isn't. This is about helping managers see what isn't there but could be— seeing the opportunities in the "white space." This is about helping managers approach their work without the fear that forms the stress that causes the unhappiness that keeps the manager from thinking clearly that causes the manager to underperform and creates more stress and fear, etc. Zen is very much about removing all the barriers we've constructed that inhibit thinking clearly.

"Okay, okay! Give me an example."

Okay. The following situation happens every day. A manager is in his boss's office and the boss starts challenging some work that the manager has done. The manager gets defensive and a little flustered (because of past bad encounters with this boss, or worse, some prior boss) and fails to explain things properly. The meeting ends badly. The manager goes back to his office and then realizes what he should have said. He knew the exact right thing to say, but he just didn't say it. And the reason he didn't come up with it in his boss's office is that his mind was blocked by the emotional barriers created by being challenged by his boss. (He'd been bitten by a "manager" dog in the past.) Sound familiar?

"Been there, done that. So how would Zen help?"

Zen will help knock down those emotional barriers. Remember, you brought those emotional barriers into your boss's office with you. You also brought the right answers in with you.

Let's start with what are called **The Three Treasures:**

- Buddha existed and everyone has a Buddha nature inside waiting to be brought forth.
- The dharma, the teachings of Buddha, are ultimate truth.
- Man is both unique and part of everything.

Within the dharma are the **Four Noble Truths:**

- Within life there is pain and unhappiness, discontent, and dissatisfaction, "weltschmerz." This is *dukkha*. It is the barrier to joy and fulfillment. It is the mind trapped in negativistic spiraling.
- Suffering—dukkha—is caused by desire, wanting things one doesn't have.
- Take away the desire for what one doesn't have and the suffering goes away (this doesn't mean one can't enjoy things or love people, it is not setting a limit on joy—it means one has to surrender the need to have something, the clinging to a passion, the grasping of what cannot be grasped).
- Happiness is found by following the "Eightfold Path"—eight steps that provide guidelines to living a balanced life (the genesis of the Code of the Samurai can easily be found here).

The Eightfold Path

- **Right Understanding:** Understanding the Four Noble Truths, the realness of Karma, and the unity of things.
- **Right Thinking:** Thinking positively and avoiding the base, cruel, and immoral thoughts.
- **Right Speech:** Not lying, not gossiping, not talking too much—speaking wisely, with kindness.
- **Right Action:** Acting morally.
- **Right Livelihood:** Avoiding work that supports immorality, hurting people, or victimizing others. Do work that helps others.
- **Right Effort:** Being your best self, emphasizing positive qualities, exercising self-control.
- **Right Mindfulness:** Being fully aware of what is occurring inside and outside of oneself, using one's mind fully without barriers.
- **Right Concentration:** Fully concentrating on what one is doing, free of distracting thoughts, immersing oneself in the actions of the moment.

Like the Code of the Samurai, Zen focuses on the wholeness of being. It takes a very holistic approach that both emphasizes "doing good" and "being good," plus using one's mind to see past appearances and shallow perceptions. Both the Code and the Eightfold Path share an awareness of the fundamental interdependencies of actions and thoughts. More than any other major religion, Zen promotes improving and altering the mechanics of thinking. Note that four of the elements of the Eightfold Path are concerned with the workings of the mind. Meditation is practiced not as a form of worship, but rather as an exercise in disciplining the mind— the mental equivalent of weightlifting to improve one's body.

The Eightfold path is the rough equivalent to Christianity's Ten Commandments. Note how different these sets of guidelines are. The Ten Commandments are much more specific and prescriptive; they are very particular about what one is supposed to do or not do. The Eightfold Path, equally concerned about promoting moral behavior, is much less exact, leaving it up to the individual to conclude what the appropriate action is to take. Rather than objectifying or defining virtues and vices—rather than setting rules—it teaches a path, the Way, to enlightenment where the differences between right action and wrong action are obvious to the individual.

In a world of increasing complexity, it is impossible for any set of fixed rules to govern all possible circumstances. Knowing this, Zen focuses on the mental process of coming to the right answers based on the belief that within every individual is a fundamental wisdom, a fundamental awareness of right and wrong—the individual's True Self—that is perfectly capable of making all the right decisions all the time. That's Enlightenment, that's the Buddha nature inside us, waiting to be uncovered.

Does This Really Work?

"Wait a minute! Are you saying that the average person—the average manager—has perfect wisdom inside him or herself, just waiting to come out? You should see my manager, that guy's an idiot!"

Okay, some people's pathways to enlightenment are going to be longer than others.

"Easy for you to joke—you don't have to work for the guy!"

Okay, what's he like?

"Like I said...He's a jerk. He goes around yelling at everyone, he thinks he knows everything. He hasn't been making his sales numbers and he blames everyone else! We're just all waiting for him to get fired— but he must have pictures on somebody high up because so far he's Teflon man! He used to be a good guy...but he really seems to have lost it!"

This manager can be saved.

If this manager can accept and adopt the core intellectual precepts of Zen, he can fix the two biggest problems he has as a manager: his fearfulness and his bad judgment. Fix the fearfulness and you fix the anger that drives the yelling and the poor people skills. Fear always lurks underneath anger. Anger erupts when an individual fears losing something that is important to him or her. If the manager weren't afraid, he wouldn't be yelling. Fix the way his thinking works and you fix his bad business judgments. As he makes better business judgments, he gains more self-confidence, which leads to less fear, which leads to better relationships with his coworkers, which also leads to better decisions—and what had been an increasing disintegration becomes a process of reintegration and improvement. Zen works holistically. Even this guy can become a Samurai Leader.

As stated earlier, how to achieve fearlessness and clarity of thought will be addressed in detail later, but for now, a little more of the foundation of Zen needs to be uncovered.

Karma

The concept of Karma is simple: your destiny is determined by what you do. If you do evil, evil will come to you. If you do good, you will be rewarded. Most religions preach that doing good and doing evil have consequences. Both Western and Eastern religions agree that good is rewarded and evil is punished. The when and the how vary significantly. Since this book is not about religion, there will be no discussion of how one's actions in this life may affect what happens to that person in an afterlife or future lives. However, it could be a mistake to ignore the more immediate consequences of one's actions, especially in a business context.

As some people put it, "Karma can be a bitch!" Others like to say, "What goes around, comes around." "You get back what you put out there." The Bible puts it simply, "Whatsoever a man soweth, that shall he also reap."

A Samurai Leader respects Karma. By understanding that those who would victimize others tend to become victims themselves, the samurai manager sees that the mean-spirited takers end up unhappy and unsuccessful—Karma isn't necessarily fast acting, but it is usually very thorough.

The key point here is not about punishing the malefactors. The cool thing is that those who always try to do the right thing are the ones who are the happiest, even in the very tough business environment of today. The good one carries out really does come back pretty quickly.

In Hinduism and Buddhism, Karma is believed to be both inevitable and exacting. What one does to others comes back to that person. It acts literally as one of their laws of the universe. In most Western minds, Karma is more ambiguous; many believe it exists in more of a random state, yet recognize that it may not be safe to ignore it. As usual, in Zen, Karma is not well defined but its reality is not in question. Adhering to the Eightfold Path will lead a person to happiness and success. As a product of Zen, adhering to the Samurai Code—adjusted for management— will lead to a more joyful experience of life. That in turn will lead to less stress and greater clarity of mind. The Samurai Leader wins. Living a life where good Karma is created is just a better way of being.

Sword
Strokes

CREATING A "GOOD KARMA" TEAM

Smart managers know how to create the likelihood of good Karma occurring in a timely manner. One way is to identify individuals at one's workplace with whom one creates a musketeer relationship. ("One for all and all for one!") Ideally, these individuals should be talented and trustworthy and should be at all levels of the organization. These individuals, either formally or informally, help each other succeed in the company. They exchange information, they provide advice and sounding boards, they watch each other's backs, and they say good things about each other to powerful third parties whenever the opportunity arises. They help each other get promotions.

The key to a successful network is choosing individuals who understand how difficult it is to succeed on one's own. Everyone needs help. Networks like this are obviously valuable to the junior-most members, but they are also valuable to the highest-ranking ones. The higher one rises in an organization, the harder it is to know what is happening at ground level. Truth gets distorted and ignored. Whether working at the top or the bottom of an organization, getting the right information at the right time can be the difference between winning and losing.

People at all levels of an organization can be helpful—they will more likely help you if you help them!

Like most things in Zen, the concept of Karma is more intuitive than mystical. Good deeds tend to be rewarded and bad deeds punished. In the microcosm of a particular business environment, the results of Karma are evident over the long term. Whether that term is applied or not, business IOUs are usually repaid and revenge for past wrongs is usually exacted. That's Karma at work.

You Are Not in Control

The universe is a very, very, very big place. At that scale, an individual doesn't even register as a dust mote. Even on our little world, we are only one of billions of others. Think of the ZILLIONS (that's a really big number) of potential interactions that can occur in any given day to any particular person that can dramatically change a life. How much control do you think you have over earthquakes, hurricanes, airplanes falling out of the sky, fires, floods, murderous killing sprees, or terrorist actions? Can you control those things?

All right, those are all newspaper headline grabbing things—most of them don't happen to people you know. But what about economic downturns, new competitive threats, volatile markets, shifts in consumer tastes, changing technologies leading to product obsolescence, management changes, deaths in the family, car accidents, cancer, and heart attacks? Still think you are in control?

What about the challenge of getting subordinates to do what they need to do? What about senior management's ability to come up with the right strategies and execute? What about the capital markets properly evaluating your company's business prospects? Under control?

What about all the little things that screw things up? What about traffic jams, airplane delays, babysitters who don't show up, lost cell phones, computer viruses, the flu, car problems? Controlling those too?

The point is that our sense of control is an illusion. It is one of the lies that our minds have been taught to tell us out of egotism.

The problem is that illusion of control increases powerlessness. When these uncontrollable events or the consequences of these events occur, too many managers get upset and angry—they lose their cool— and they react badly, unproductively. Why do they do that? For the same reason a spoiled child throws a tantrum when he doesn't get his way—lack of discipline. A mind needs to learn discipline too, just like any other organism.

Let's put it simply: **Getting angry over things one can't control is stupid!**

Zen assumes this lack of control as a constant state of existence. Rather than fight the towering waves of life, it preaches how to surf them. Buddha in his flash of perfect insight did not see how to change the forces of nature and the world. He saw how to change the way to react to them to end the suffering that they so often produced.

Sword
Strokes

SURRENDERING CONTROL

Many managers confuse control with power. They believe that to be powerful they have to be able to control things—but control by its nature limits freedom of action and therefore restricts upside potential (though it may succeed at limiting downside risk.) Managers that emphasize control essentially put brakes on the growth of the units they manage.

The challenge is to surrender control while maintaining direction. "Direction" here means literally ensuring that everyone is going in the right direction. The best leaders set the strategy and empower their teams to make it happen. Empowering means:

- selecting the right members for the team;
- ensuring everyone understands their mission;
- developing individual capabilities;
- providing necessary tools and resources;
- motivating peak performance; and
- rewarding accomplishment.

> Top managers understand that these actions constitute a continuous cycle of improvement where the team's actions become less and less controlled—which gives the leader the opportunity to lead larger and larger groups, thus enabling his or her promotion! Those leaders that insist on controlling their teams essentially limit their own promotion opportunities.
>
> *The more power a manager effectively gives away, the more power that manager has!*

There Is Only Now

Not only are you not in control, but there also is no past and there is no future. This is a very fundamental concept in Zen and it is not intuitive.

Oftentimes in trying to understand Zen, it is easier to see the negation of it. Who wants to be the person who only talks about the good times he used to have in high school—constantly trying to relive those moments? Who wants to be the person who only talks about what he is going to do in the future—constantly trying to revel in future glory?

In both those cases, they are ignoring the present to live in a time that doesn't exist. Whether it did exist or will exist (an interesting philosophical conundrum) doesn't change the fact that it does not exist now and that they cannot live in those other times. One can only live in the present. Zen requires an intense focus on the actions of the moment. When a Zen master works in a garden, he is not thinking about building a new monastery or about a lecture he will be giving the next day or about what he will be eating later. He is experiencing the texture of the soil, the green of the leaves, the blueness of the sky, and the smell of the fertilizer—all of his awareness is centered on just the experience of gardening.

This isn't to say the Zen master doesn't address the needs of the future. At one moment in time, he planned what to raise in his garden so that he would have something to eat in the coming winter. When he was involved in planning what would be raised in the garden, all of his thought and attention were focused on that—in the same fully mentally committed way that he experienced his time with spade or hoe in hand.

At no point in anyone's life will they live in any other moment, past or future, than the moment they are in. This is not to say that NOW is static, unchanging. NOW is constantly changing and evolving. Part of living in the NOW involves preparing for how NOW will change.

"Okay, okay. Fine! That's just a mind game kind of thing. Why do I care? How is that going to make me a better manager?"

Remember all those things that can't be controlled? Remember all those bad things that happened as a result of those events? None of them are happening NOW. They are not part of this moment. Why carry them with you? That is needless pain. Why let them dull your mind, depress your emotions, dampen your spirit? Let go of old failures! None of them are happening NOW.

Sword

Strokes

EXECUTING THE PLAN

Execution of a strategy or plan of work is all about taking action NOW. The time for debating the merits of objectives and approaches ended with the formalization of the strategy or plan. Once it's time to implement, full commitment is essential. Good execution demands that everyone charged with delivering the plan focus on the doing of it. There should be no second guessing, no carrying forward of old experiences (good or bad), no looking ahead to future developments. Fear of failure must be surrendered.

Each member of the team needs to:

- have their role and expectations clearly identified;
- have the actions they are supposed to take clearly described;
- have appropriate measurements and rewards of success established;
- have milestones set; and
- get to work!

Once it is time to act, everyone's frame of mind should be centered on NOW!

"So I'm just supposed to forget about all those bad things that happened to me? Just get to work."

Not forget, just set them aside. You do not need to dwell on them—that's just your mind wanting attention. They have nothing to do with the moment you are in. Remember, those things weren't under your control. They happened. By carrying them with you into each new NOW, you let them continue to happen.

"But they still hurt."

Acknowledge the pain. Examine the pain. It's there, right now, so recognize it for what it is. And then ignore it. Give it no more attention. It's mental background static and it must be filtered out. Permitting these old bad events to continue in your current emotional/ mental environment is like bringing a computer virus into a healthy software program. It corrupts the system and blocks it from functioning properly. Clarity of thought and action is lost.

"So how am I supposed to do that? Believe me, I've tried."

It's not like you fix one thing and you're done. It doesn't work that way at the corporate level and it doesn't work that way at the individual level. Zen approaches this much more holistically. There is the Eightfold Path to be followed, your True Self to be acknowledged, the surrendering of attachments to be accomplished, and the Way to perfect insight to be traveled. Future chapters will tie these actions together in the context of the needs of a Samurai Leader. But for now, one other part of Zen needs to be mentioned.

Meditation

The word "Zen" means "meditation" in Japanese. *Zazen* means "sitting meditation." For some Zen practitioners, meditation is the doorway to the mindfulness that becomes the awareness of the True Self. Others believe it is the Way itself, that only while in meditation is there the mindfulness that sees true reality. Certainly without meditation, it is extremely difficult to master the mindfulness that is at the heart of Zen.

For the Samurai Leader, you don't need to take meditation to its full potential. This book isn't a treatise on Zen. However, like other elements of Zen, meditation can be used as a tool to raise the level of a manager's game. At a minimum, the development of the mental discipline inherent in practicing meditation will pay dividends to a manager seeking to make the right decisions amidst the bedlam of too much data and too many distractions in today's corporate world. What follows is a practical view of how to approach meditation to gain some of its effectiveness.

Think of meditation as the equivalent of taking a time-out during a basketball or football game. When the game is on the line and things aren't going quite right, it's a good idea often to just stop and give yourself a chance to regroup and calm down—to regain your focus on what you are trying to do. You don't have to do it, but you'll probably play better if you do. Also, you've probably noticed that not all athletes handle time-outs the same. Some reach for towels or water bottles, some just sit down—but all are seeking more calm and clarity. And usually the coaches are just telling his players to settle down, focus on the basics.

Meditation can be done a lot of different ways, whatever works. You can do it alone or with other people. You can sit still in the lotus position or walk around the neighborhood. You can chant a mantra, count your breaths, listen to jazz, or stare at the shadings of darkness when your eyes are closed. It's up to you.

The goal is for a little while each day, for your mind to be still—no racing thoughts forcing their way into the front of your consciousness. Whatever it is you choose to focus upon, keep your attention there, not through an intense fixation, but rather with a calm and steadfast intention. If wandering thoughts intrude, acknowledge their presence, then return to the center of your focus. Experience the NOWness of it. Feel the moment as if it is all there is. Nothing exists outside of it. Don't use this time to solve problems. This is not a time to think. This is a time of Not Thinking!

Meditation can be done anywhere and at any time. Obviously, some places and some times are better than others. It needs to fit into each person's life in a way that matches his or her environment and schedule. If five minutes are all that are available, then just take five. More time will be more helpful, but in this, every little bit helps. It can be especially useful in times of intense commotion like a mini business crisis of the type that seems to occur almost weekly in today's hectic business world. When in the midst of one of those times, take a ten-minute time-out and a walk outside—and don't think about anything in particular. Just look at the trees or the clouds. Then get back to work. You'll be better because of those ten minutes of meditation.

Whole books are written just about how to meditate and certainly some adherents think their ways are best. Maybe they are—who knows? The point is, this doesn't hurt and it does help, for almost everyone. It is just about taking some time out to get your mind back in sync with the rest of the program. It is a way of rebooting to cleanse some system errors or to affect system readjustment. The mind, like a piece of software, may instruct the actions of its host, but it is not the host itself. Like a piece of software, the program can degrade or be subject to faulty algorithms. It needs to be refreshed. Your mind is not you.

It is not your mind's fault. During most of its millions of years of evolution, one of its primary purposes was to identify threats and then determine whether to fight or flee. This orientation around threat identification followed by the "fight or flight" decision was critical to survival for a man facing saber-toothed tigers and mastodons. However, its utility in the modern world is much less essential and in many instances counterproductive.

It is a result of the mind's preference (think "hard wired") for a fight or flight decision that too often managers facing a perceived threat do in fact fight or flee. They make a bad decision when neither of those actions are optimal to the situation. In such circumstances, the Samurai Leader needs to quiet his or her mind's knee-jerk preference and instill a mental discipline to examine the threat first and then determine the optimum course of action. That mental discipline can be achieved through meditation.

Koans

A koan is a story, a question, a paradox, or an anecdote that seems illogical or nonsensical as it is first understood. In Zen, they are tools to unravel the traditional knitting of our minds to foster a deeper understanding. They are not meant to develop a superior logic; just the opposite, they are used to illuminate an awareness of life's intricacies that no logic can approach.

An example: A monk asked a Zen master, "How can one escape the cold and the heat?"

The Zen Master replied, "Why not go where there is no cold and no heat?"

The monk asked, "Is there such a place?"

The master replied, "When it's cold, be cold. When it's hot, be hot."

Samurai understood this koan. In fact, they used it as a guide to limit physical discomfort. The mind only knows discomfort to the extent it pays attention to the messages the body is sending it. And the message the body is sending is, "Do something, I don't like this!" But what if the mind says, "Relax, it's only pain, let's know it for what it is, then let's go through it until we are past it. Then I'm going to ignore it."

Other koans include:

- "What is the sound of one hand clapping?"
- "What is the mind doing when it is not thinking?"
- "How can you proceed from the top of a hundred foot pole?"

The important point here is that every manager can be a better manager by shedding preconceptions, focusing more deeply, and acting consistently with the Code of the Samurai or the Eightfold Path. For now, perhaps, you need to take that on faith. But remember this: the Samurai Code worked very well for over seven hundred years in Japan. Zen Buddhism has been developing for over twenty-five hundred years across all of Asia. All this book is aiming at is to present the "Greatest Hits" of a samurai/Zen combination.

So here is all you have to take on faith:

- You are capable of much better thinking.
- You are capable of being fearless.
- You are capable of being much happier.

QUESTIONS TO CONSIDER

1. What business occurrences in your past do you need to forget about in order to become a better leader?

2. What parts of your business do you believe you really control?

Two Business Koans:

1. When is the leader the servant?

2. What profit is not profitable?

CHAPTER SIX

COURAGE AND FEARLESSNESS
PART I:
THE WAY OF ACTING

Who wouldn't want to be fearless? All the best superheroes are. Of course, having super powers is a big advantage. It makes that whole fearlessness thing a lot easier. But for those without super powers, true fearlessness is difficult to even imagine. So many people carry so many fears around so constantly that the fears become the background static to our existence, the grayness that pales the vibrant colors of our life. We accept our fears as a natural part of the human condition. In business, fear is omnipresent, but no one ever talks about it—it's bad politics to admit to it.

A samurai goes to battle fearlessly.

A Samurai Leader manages fearlessly.

A SAMURAI LEADER STORY

(Names have been changed)

When Steve took over as CEO, the company was heading toward bankruptcy. The management team wasn't working well together, the employees were unhappy, and the customers were deserting. Steve was determined to rise to the challenge. He knew everyone was counting on him. He knew, too, that some thought he didn't have enough experience to succeed (he was pretty young). He resolved to give it everything he had. He set to work.

Within three years, he had turned the company around. Everyone thought he had done a terrific job. The employees loved him. They appreciated his friendly, open style, and that he always was supportive and encouraging. His managers respected and admired him for how he had built up the team and led them through the tough times. At the end of that third year, the company reported record financial results. Everyone was excited about the company's future under Steve's leadership. Steve was everyone's hero.

Steve killed himself soon after that.

Everyone was shocked. No one had seen it coming. No one had thought he was depressed, let alone suicidal. No one except his wife. She had seen how he had felt the weight of the company on his shoulders and how afraid he was that he couldn't continue to make the right decisions. He was afraid he couldn't keep up with everyone's expectations, which were higher and higher every day. He had hidden that fear day after day, but with each success, the burden became heavier. Finally, he couldn't take it anymore.

The workday fears that most managers have don't usually result in self-destructive action as extreme as in Steve's case. But there are many instances of managers behaving in ways that are self-destructive where the underlying driver is their need to get out of a situation that is too stressful. It's just too hot to stay in the kitchen. Oftentimes, the self-destruction comes through alcoholism or drug dependency, but sometimes the symptoms are not as obvious. Sometimes it's the explanation for why smart people do dumb things—why so often in people's careers they figuratively shoot their own feet off. They don't even know they are doing it. The manager's behavior just isn't explainable any other way. The mind figures out a way to get out of the kitchen—it can't take it anymore.

Yet most managers are so accustomed to the fears they carry—fears of being fired, fears of not making their numbers, fears of not being respected by their peers, fears of losing a big customer or a big deal—that they cannot even imagine their world without the fear. They accept their sleepless nights, their gastrointestinal diseases, waves of panic, and wired emotions, as the natural consequences of making a living. They don't even call it fear. It's just stress. After all, it's a battle out there, there are going to be casualties.

The casualties of fear are many. Fear kills and maims. It does not usually do so dramatically, but invariably and with an arsenal of weapons like heart attacks, stress disorders, depression—the list here too is long. And its victims are not just the ones who are afraid. Their families and coworkers feel the results of that fear—the angers, the self-destructive behavior, the joylessness.

"Nobody wants to be afraid. But what can you do?"

Actually, you can do a lot. It's time to get rid of the fear.

A Samurai and the Idea of Death

A samurai awoke in the morning with the idea of his death and carried it with him all day. Yet, he still loved life! Life was precious to him, too, the more so because death could be so close. He understood that his death defined his life, made the moments irreplaceable and not to be squandered heedlessly. And he understood that at the time of his death he would be judged by how well he embraced it.

Just as a samurai, to function at his best, had to daily accept the idea of his death, in the same way, a manager must daily accept losing his job.

A manager must fearlessly view job loss, must accept that at any time he could be terminated at work, and that nothing could be more ignominious than to act dishonestly, disreputably, or cowardly out of fear of being fired. For a manager to do his best work, to love the challenges of a business career where paradigms shift with apparent reckless abandon, a manager cannot fear dying in battle; he cannot fear losing his job!

"Not be afraid of losing your job—are you nuts?!"

It can be done. A samurai did not want to die, but he gave up his fear of dying. The fear itself was self-defeating. For a manager, acting fearfully all the time is far more likely to result in termination at work than acting fearlessly all the time. Fear promotes wild emotional responses. It blocks clarity of thought. It blocks creativity. It inhibits leadership. It restricts good managers. In business, it is the ultimate counterproductive way of being. And it is a way of being! It comes from inside a person. To do away with fear, to rid oneself of stress, one must change one's relationship to those things and events that cause the fear.

A samurai's adherence to the Code of the Samurai facilitated his acting bravely. His Zen beliefs facilitated fearlessness. The Samurai Code offers a clear and convincing guide to drive the actions that a manager must take to succeed. Thus, the fear of doing the wrong thing is dissipated. Additionally, Zen helped samurai detach from anticipated consequences—by showing that the negative consequences one anticipates are no more real than the positive consequences one hopes for based on other actions. The world is way too complex for anyone to know the long-term likely consequences of any particular set of actions. "Do your best now—and then don't worry about it."

Though at times it seems contagious, one can build up an immunity to fear. It starts by acting as if one is not afraid, even though one's hands may be shaking. The right thing gets done despite the fear. That's courage.

Fearlessness is better. But to get to fearlessness you must change your way of being, not just your way of acting. For most managers, losing one's job is the most frightful of all possible events. One can face it courageously, but in order to excel at one's job, one must give up the fear of losing it! Ironic, isn't it?

COURAGE AND FEARLESSNESS PART I

Fear and Stress

Corporate America is consumed by fear. But the word "fear" is unattractive, so it has been replaced by the more politically correct term "stress." Managers who would never admit to being afraid will admit to being "over-stressed." But it is just fear by another name. Most of that stress is related to job performance. Underlying that is the fear of losing one's job. (That's why taking a vacation not only doesn't relieve the stress, it may actually make it worse!) Overcoming the fear associated with losing one's job is the most challenging barrier to becoming a Samurai Leader.

To calmly accept being fired at work in the same way a samurai accepts dying in battle is a daunting psychological readjustment for most managers. The older the manager and the more he or she is tied financially, socially and personally to a particular organization, the harder it gets. For many, that kind of fearlessness will seem unachievable. But by carrying the fear inside, the manager limits his or her potential and increases the likelihood of ultimately being involuntarily terminated. Fear limits creativity. Fear blocks rational thought. Fear engenders anger. Fear kills.

Losing Your Fear

There is no one easy thing to do that will take away fear. If there were, you'd have done it. Rather, it takes a combination of things: a way of acting plus a way of thinking. Samurai practiced both.

Courage is measured by the action one takes in the face of adversity and threats. The key word here is action—one has to act. In Shakespeare's great play *Hamlet,* paralyzed by doubt as to whether his father the king was actually murdered by Hamlet's uncle, Hamlet goes through most of the play being a pain to everyone, especially himself. It might be a great work of drama and a terrific role to play, but who would want to *be* Hamlet?

Hamlet's problem is he doesn't know what to do. He needs to make a decision. His decision was whether to kill his stepfather, the new king, or not. Fortunately, most managers don't have to make life and death decisions. The key here is that not making a decision is actually far more stressful than making one. Even if it comes down to flipping a coin, **flip the coin!**

Acting Right

Okay, you are ready to act, but what do you do? What would a samurai do? That's easy. A samurai would act in accordance with the Code of the Samurai! That's what the code is there for. The Code is essential for two primary reasons:

1. The Code provides a framework for determining the correct action to be taken.

2. Adherence to the Code will result in the "right" (as in righteous, as in morally correct) action to be taken.

"But what does this have to do with courage and fearlessness?"

A lot! When you *know* you are acting "in the right," it is much easier, much less stressful, to take action. Fear dissipates when one is certain of the rightness of one's actions.

"But what if the decision to be made isn't about doing what's right. It's like whether you should go to the left or to the right. Just a pure business decision. How does the Samurai Code or Zen help me from being afraid about making the wrong business decision?"

Several ways. They will help you approach the issues with greater mental calm; a racing mind doesn't think clearly. Equally important, they'll help you separate the decision from its consequences. Some bad decisions turn out well, and some good decisions turn out badly. You really are not in control of many of the determining factors. Furthermore, life is so complicated that fearing a particular result is to ignore the unimaginable chains of events where failures lead to successes and successes lead to failures—

that is the norm in everyone's life. Just do your best...and then accept what comes.

"Are you saying that the decisions I make don't really matter? That's not true. A lot of times the decisions I make turn out just like I wanted them to."

I'm sure that's true, but it's not the point. Let's look at an example. Joe, a middle manager at a widget company gets a promotion to vice president (that's good), works for a new boss who doesn't like Joe, and six months later Joe gets fired (that's bad). But Joe gets a job offer that pays more than his old job (that's good). Soon after starting, Joe is involved in a car accident and breaks his leg on his way to his new office (that's bad). While in the hospital, he meets a nurse and they fall in love and get married (that's good) and Joe and the nurse live happily ever after—all because Joe got fired. That's how our lives work—none of us know what is really going to follow from decisions we make or things that happen to us, so why always fear the worst?

A SAMURAI LEADER STORY

In December 1990, when Bill was general counsel of SystemOne, a subsidiary of Continental Airlines, the airline was days away from filing bankruptcy and was desperate for cash. All executives were challenged to come up with capital every possible way. The problem was that all the sources of capital were aware that Continental was about to file for bankruptcy and knew that doing anything before the filing could have the effect of just throwing their money away.

As SystemOne was building a relationship with EDS, it was determined to try to work out some kind of deal there. In the space of three days, Bill, without assistance from anyone else (because he could do it faster if no one else was involved), negotiated a loan agreement with EDS for thirty-five million dollars. That alone was a superior piece of work, but the problem was only half solved. The thirty-five million was sitting in SystemOne's bank account, but Bill had to get the money up to Continental. The airline's CFO demanded that Bill issue the bank instructions to wire the money into Continental's accounts. Bill refused on the basis that unless the proper deal was struck between Continental and SystemOne, it would be a fraudulent conveyance, defrauding the creditors of SystemOne (which was also going to be drawn into Continental's bankruptcy filing).

The airline's CFO offered a deal he thought was sufficient and then demanded again that the money be sent. Bill again refused on the basis that the deal offered by the airline was not adequate. The CFO (at that time the person really running the airline) threatened to fire Bill unless he did what he was told. The CEO of SystemOne was leaving it all on Bill. Time was now very short—the filing was to take place in less than forty-eight hours.

Bill consulted several outsiders in whom he had great trust and determined what the necessary terms of the deal between Continental and SystemOne needed to be. He made up his mind what the deal had to be in order to meet the needs of both the airline and its subsidiary. A meeting was held. The CFO once again demanded the money be wired to the airline on the terms the airline set. When Bill refused, the CFO cursed Bill and again threatened to fire him. Calmly Bill laid out the deal he would agree to. Finally, the deal was struck on the terms Bill laid out. The documents were quickly prepared and hours before Continental's filing for chapter 11, the thirty-five million dollars were wired into the airline's bank account. Bill fully expected to be fired the next day.

Bill was not fired. The thirty-five million was hugely important in helping the airline get through the first few days of bankruptcy—it had been truly out of cash. Without the money

*from SystemOne, Continental probably would
not have survived intact. The deal on the thirty-
five million was very closely examined by the
bankruptcy court and was determined to be
fair and reasonable and not a fraudulent conveyance. Continental not only survived, but
also became very successful and highly
respected. The CFO was promoted to CEO of
the Airline. When soon thereafter the CEO of
SystemOne left the company, the CFO, now
CEO of the airline, promoted Bill to CEO of
SystemOne and made him a member of his
senior executive team.*

The key to understanding Bill's actions in this
Samurai Leader situation is that under circumstances
of enormous pressure, with potentially the fate of
both the airline and the subsidiary riding on him—
plus the reality of being fired—Bill *knew* he was
doing the right thing. He had consulted the people
he believed could give him the best possible advice,
then he acted on what he and his advisors had con-
cluded. He accepted the consequences, whatever
they might be.

There is real power in acting in accordance with
one's beliefs. The corollary of that is also true: when
one's actions are not consistent with beliefs, one loses

that sense of conviction—and distress and failure follow. In the Oscar-winning movie *Chariots of Fire,* one of the runners was devoutly religious and believed his running was in the service of God. When confronted with having to run a race on Sunday, which he believed would have been a breach of the Sabbath, he could not run. He would have lost his power to run fast.

In both the Code of the Samurai and in Zen's Eightfold Path, the importance of the right action cannot be overstated. Fearlessness is as much a requirement for the Zen master as it is for the samurai. In both cases, experiencing fear would be a barrier to attaining their respective ways of being. For them, even having courage isn't enough because courage is a matter of overcoming fears that continue to exist. What is required is a totally fearless mind. Without a fearless mind, the samurai cannot achieve his sense of oneness with the battle and the Zen master cannot achieve true mindfulness.

The samurai *knew* that if his actions were in all cases consistent with the whole of the Code, then there was nothing to fear. His actions were compelled by the Code and nothing bad could follow from that. Fear could only enter if he did not adhere to the Code. In the same way, as a Samurai Leader truly embraces and adheres to a Samurai Leader Code, doubt and fears will begin to fall away.

Sword

Strokes

BUILDING A SUPPORT TEAM

To successfully climb the corporate ladder, one needs to rely on the expertise of others. There is just too much to know for any one person to master all the competencies required. In the course of just a year's time, most managers can expect challenging issues requiring some knowledge of law, accounting, financial management, technology, human resources, and career planning. The mix of these issues will depend, of course, on the specifics of the manager's responsibilities— and there are probably other areas of expertise that will also be necessary. The point is that there is way too much to know—far too much to look to one's mentor (if one even has one) for the answers.

A wise manager assembles an unofficial "dream team" of experts. Don't just rely on the "official" experts that your company offers up. Some of them may be good, but others won't be. Also, they will have their own interests to protect and enhance. Your interests will be subservient to theirs. You need your own experts.

The trick here is to identify and nurture them before you need them. Do something for them first. Make them want to help you when the time comes. Flatter them. Most of the individuals that really know what they are doing will happily give their advice if properly approached—and you really listen. Then conform their advice to your needs. By listening to the people who really get it, and who are not tied to the specific issues personally, you can become more certain that you are doing the right thing. That will give you more confidence in your decision.

Make friends with the gurus!

A SAMURAI LEADER STORY

A number of years ago Eastern Airlines decided it was time to change the look of its flight attendants' uniform. After consulting with fashion designers, airline executives, and union leaders, agreement was reached on a new uniform. It had a quite distinctive militaristic look and was a dark olive green, an unusual color for a flight attendant uniform of the day. Tony (not his real name), the manager in the airline's purchasing department who had administered the uniform selection process, carried forward the uniform change so that by the scheduled day thousands of flight attendants all had their new uniforms. Everything went according to plan. But there turned out to be a problem. The flight attendants themselves didn't like the look. Even worse, neither did most of the passengers!

As the unpopularity of the uniforms became known, the CEO of the airline grew furious! He called Walt, the vice president of purchasing, into his office and told Walt (who had nothing to do with the uniform selection) to go and fire Tony because of the way the uniforms had turned out. Before firing Tony, Walt conducted an investigation and learned that although Tony had administered the process—and was not entirely blameless—Tony had not been the decision maker as to the look of the uniform. The CEO had voiced his opinion—and so had the CEO's wife—in favor of the chosen design. Tony had really just followed orders.

Walt went back to the CEO and told him that he did not believe that Tony's actions warranted being fired. The CEO would not accept that as an answer and ordered Walt to fire Tony. Walt repeated that Tony should not be fired. The CEO screamed at Walt to go and fire Tony or he would fire Walt for not firing Tony. Walt still refused. The CEO then fired Walt, who had worked for the airline for over twenty years.

As things turned out, a powerful member of the board of directors argued on behalf of Walt and managed to get Walt rehired. Tony also ended up keeping his job.

A couple of years later, Walt retired. A retirement party was held and people who had worked with Walt over the years came to honor him. They came from France and Germany, they came from Australia, they came from everywhere! And there were a lot of them! Everyone wanted to honor this man who throughout his career, as testimonial after testimonial made clear, had always acted honorably, courageously, and to the highest standard of integrity.

As one who was at Walt's retirement party remembers, from all the stories that were told, it was clear that the courage and honor that Walt exhibited in dealing with the uniform situation had been exhibited throughout his career and led to many of his successes. People wanted to do business with him.

Training to Be Fearless

So—the first key to fearlessness is **do the right thing!**

Samurai took training very seriously. Training had two major components. Constant practice in the martial arts was a daily regimen. Their skill with the long and the short sword and the other weapons of battle was of life and death importance. Secondly, personal physical fitness was both a matter of pride as well as survival. Both of those elements of training contributed to the fearlessness of the samurai.

The link between training and fearlessness is not an outmoded idea. Every major military in the world understands the importance of training, both as to weapons as well as to physical conditioning. Good training and conditioning leads to a confident soldier, and confidence is one of the keys to courage and fearlessness. A soldier who is not confident in his abilities is a liability to the others who will need to rely on him.

Good training is no less important for a manager. Great companies like GE and IBM invest heavily in management training and managers need to look for ways to take advantage of training opportunities offered by their companies. Competency requirements do not remain fixed; constant improvement is a necessity. The better the company, the more true this becomes. Leaders must continually upgrade their management skills; their followers will expect it of them. Without growth, their message will soon sound tired and worn out. Technology changes in particular are driving changes in managers' skill sets. Failing to embrace the new technologies would be like the samurai who failed to take advantage of muskets in the early seventeenth century and fought those guns just with their swords. They died.

Nothing is more debilitating than fear of incompetence. Being a superior manager requires a mastery of the management tools available. Those tools vary based on the management situations involved, but you know what is needed. Maintaining skills is obviously important, especially where technology innovations are happening every day. Keep up! Fear will dog the laggards!

The necessity of training to enhance management skills doesn't need much explaining here, but from the evidence visible at management meetings and forums, the importance of physical fitness probably does need emphasis. Skipping over all the obvious reasons to keep fit (you know them already), here's a truth that is perhaps not as obvious. Being physically fit leads directly to a greater feeling of confidence, which itself leads to less fear.

The job market is highly competitive and anyone in it who appears confident and physically fit has a real advantage over those who don't. Our culture is extremely "looks" oriented and anyone who looks out of shape is at a disadvantage against those who look fit. The cool thing here is that so many managers are out of shape that it is easy to stand out. Of course, there are the other obvious advantages to a manager, such as more endurance and ability to focus. But the main point here is that in order to be more fearless, one's fitness matters. The better you feel about yourself, the less threatened you'll feel from being thrown into the job market. The more confident you feel about surviving in the job market, the less you will fear losing your job and the more fearless you will be. Maintain that fighting edge!

So another key to fearlessness—**training matters!**

QUESTIONS TO CONSIDER

1. Have you ever faced a situation where doing what was right could work against you? What did you do? What happened? Did you make a good decision?

2. Do you present yourself well physically? What are the costs to you of not doing so?

CHAPTER SEVEN

COURAGE AND FEARLESSNESS
PART II:
THE WAY OF THINKING

Fear lives in the mind. It may churn the stomach and send jagged waves of tension and energy throughout the body, but it sets up shop in the mind. As stated earlier, one of the mind's principal functions is to identify threats and then compel action—fight or flight. That fear factor that sparks the body into overdrive was really useful for the million years that fighting or fleeing were optimum decisions. The fact that fight or flight is no longer usually the optimal response hasn't yet been rewired into our minds. In fact, that response is harmful most of the time when facing the threats of the modern business world. That problem is not going to be solved here. Once your mind identifies a perceived threat, the consequences of fear are set in motion. That particular mind/body connection is out of our control.

What isn't hardwired into the mind is the identification of threats. This can be fixed! The mind's definition of what constitutes a threat can be rewritten at the individual level. And once a perceived threat is eliminated, the related fear and the consequences of that fear are eliminated as well. Even better news is that there are several ways to do the rewriting. Also, the various ways to do so are not mutually exclusive and doing even a little rewriting can make a difference. The target is not all or nothing. Fear elimination can be effective by degrees.

"Hey, you're treating fear like it's a big deal for me. I'm a pretty macho guy—I'm not running around being afraid all day. I'm cool in a crisis. I've just been feeling a lot of stress lately. That's all."

Overstressed is just the politically correct way of saying scared! We know we can't go around saying we are scared all the time. That would not be acceptable. So we call it stress. But let's be real. Where do you think stress comes from? It is just the outgrowth of fear—fear of not measuring up, fear of not being able to get the job done, fear of...etc., etc. And this isn't about how well you handle the stress. This is about getting rid of it.

How Fear Harms You

Let's start with all the everyday fears. You know the list. The fears that keep you awake at night. The worries you carry around with you all day that pop in and out of your consciousness. The things that make you bite your lip or stare off into space with the look on your face of a deer caught in headlights. The fears that churn the stomach. Those fears. But the catch is, all those bad things you worry about? **They almost never happen!**

Think about that! If you are like most people, you will spend a sizable fraction of your life worrying about things that never occur. And the reason they don't occur has got nothing to do with your having worried about them.

In fact, the more one worries about something, the more likely it is to happen. You bring substance to your fears. The golf course is a great place to see this negative force in action.

Joe is set to hit his drive on the par four, sixteenth hole. He's playing very well and has been hitting his drive down the middle all day. There is a lake down the left-hand side of the fairway but the fairway is pretty wide. Joe is standing on the tee telling himself, "Just don't hit it in the lake! Just don't hit it in the lake!" You know what he does. He hits it in the lake.

You think that just happens in golf? What about the manager about to make a presentation to the vice president of his division telling himself, "Just don't be nervous, don't be nervous." Do you think that is going to work?

Some people argue that worrying is good for them because it motivates them to do what they need to do. Sadly, this is actually true for some people. This is also the equivalent of people saying it is good to have a lion chasing them remorselessly all day because it keeps them moving.

This is nuts! Granted, action motivated by worry may be better than doing nothing all day, but there are much healthier sources of motivation. Moreover, as one approaches the work differently, the results are much better. If our golfer Joe was "in the zone," he wouldn't even see the lake, and he certainly wouldn't hit into it! The confident salesman makes the sale. The key is **banish the negative thoughts!**

Banishing Negative Thoughts

"You know, I try that—but they keep coming back. What else can I do?"

You can challenge your fears. If you are afraid of heights, make yourself go up somewhere high. If you are afraid of the water, learn how to swim. If you are afraid of public speaking, give speeches in public. Do the things you are afraid of. Fear is contagious and it spreads easily, but the reverse is true, too. As you face a fear and overcome it, other fears lose their potency. If you can't actually do the thing that you are afraid of, then at least look at it with all of its subtleties and horrors.

One of the most common examples of fear that a business leader must face occurs with a promotion or job change where all of a sudden there is a new team to lead—usually under challenging circumstances. The fear, of course, is that the new team won't be impressed with their new leader. Now most leaders know already that showing fear at that time is not helpful, but most leaders are not fully aware that what is going on in their mind is showing on their face and in their body language. If you are feeling it, it is very hard to hide it.

At such times, it is essential to stay positive! Make your first actions things you know you are good at. Look for some easy victories, even if they are little things—and don't share your fear with anyone! Instead, work at making your team feel confident. Actually, they are more afraid of you than you should be of them. As you work at erasing their fears, yours are not on display. As you succeed with making them feel more assured—surprise, surprise—you will too!

Do what a samurai did—accept that the worst thing you fear will happen that day.

Samurai had to confront the fear of death. Death was stalking them. But to show fear would have been shameful and to feel fear would have diminished their ability to survive. So instead, they were trained to wake up every morning and accept their death that day. They accustomed their minds to the idea of death. By confronting it every day, it lost its power. They embraced the vision that a heroic death would lead to their being reincarnated as a samurai again. A bad death could block that path.

A SAMURAI STORY

The Battle of Anegawa in 1570 involved almost fifty thousand soldiers, and its outcome was an important step in what would lead to the unification of Japan. The armies of Oda Nabunaga and Tokugawa Ieyasu fought against the armies of Asakura Yoshikage and Asai Nagamasa. Yet, even in such an extensive and mammoth battlefield, time would be taken out for individual duels and honor. One such singular event influenced the overall battle.

During a time of intense struggle, the commander in chief of the Asakura army was completely surrounded by the opposing forces and he and his army needed time to retreat and reform their battle lines. At this time, a samurai named Makara Jurozaemon stepped forth and volunteered to cover their withdrawal. He issued a challenge by shouting in a loud voice that he would fight anyone from the Nabunaga-Tokugawa side.

His challenge was first accepted by a samurai from an ally of Tokugawa whom Makara killed. Then, joined by his son, they repeatedly fought off attacks by a number of Tokugawa samurai while the Asakura army slowly withdrew behind them. Finally, under a simultaneous attack of four samurai while his son was otherwise engaged, and despite seriously wounding several of them, Makara was killed and decapitated. His son too was killed while trying to rejoin the departing troops. While losing their lives, they had achieved their objective and had gained the necessary time for the Asakura army to reestablish their defensive position. Makara and his son were honored by other samurai long after their deaths.

This is not to say that the samurai sought death out. They were in no hurry to meet it. But they did understand two things about death: first, by waking up to it every morning they could face it better when it did come calling; and second, it brought clarity and emphasis to the rest of their life. No moment was to be wasted.

Overcoming the fear of death isn't paramount for most managers. However, there is an equivalent fear for most managers—particularly in these days of non-stop lay-offs and headcount actions. Most managers view losing their job the same way samurai viewed losing their life. Underlying all the stress for most managers is their fear that if they don't perform and play the corporate politics correctly, their name will be on the next headcount reduction list. They fear that one bad year (or one lost big deal or one screwed up decision)—something they had no real control over—will cost them their jobs. And if they lose their job, a parade of horribles haunt them. Just like the samurai, Samurai Leaders need to get over their greatest fear!

Sword

Strokes

ACCEPTING BLAME

Sometimes things go wrong. Mistakes get made and upper management gets upset. In a complex environment, it is not always apparent who was to blame and quite often more than one person was responsible for the situation. When everyone involved is backpedaling away and claiming innocence—or worse, everyone starts pointing fingers at everyone else—the situation can further deteriorate, and the right way to deal with the problem will often get lost.

Sometimes this can create an opportunity for a manager. Rather than disclaiming responsibility or remaining silent, the right play may be to accept the mistake as yours—even when you know that it really wasn't. The reason for doing so is that it changes the political environment. If upper management is good and paying attention, they will see the acceptance of responsibility as an act of courage and an act that helps the team move forward to start dealing with the problem. In most cases, everyone really does know where the fault really lies. Additionally, the manager who steps up and takes responsibility usually also has the opportunity to frame the problem and to develop the solution. Thus, the manager not only performs damage control but also opens up the chance to be the hero. (The circumstances have to be right for this, and it can't be done too often!)

Sometimes it's wise to take the bullet for the team!

"Wait a minute. You don't know...If I lose my job, I'm in big trouble! My oldest kid's going to college and my youngest needs braces and I've got almost no savings...."

I know, I know. A lot of bad things could happen **if** you lost your job. Although it is also true that a lot of good things could happen, too. (You could find a better job, you could spend a little more time with your family, you could show your children that adversity really does happen, but that like most things, it can be endured and not be defeating—as is oft quoted, "What doesn't kill you makes you stronger.") The truth is, you don't know what would happen if you lost your job. What is certain is that carrying around the fear of losing one's job (at a low-level background moan with occasional spikes of mental shrieking) not only diminishes the joy of every day but also may contribute to the occurrence of what is feared. Furthermore, it is probably never going to happen! And if it does happen, it was probably out of your control. And even when it does happen, it is not happening NOW!

Follow the samurai's lead on this. Wake up every morning and accept you may lose your job today. For the first few mornings, examine all your thoughts around it, what you would do, how you would tell your friends and family, what you would have to change while you were job hunting. Write it all down. Write down the worst case. Be realistic. It probably looks pretty bad. Maybe instead of managing a division you'll be working as a salesman, or bartending. Guess what—you'll adjust. You will still be you. You won't be better or worse than you were before.

After you've explored this worst-case scenario daily for a while, you won't have to spend as much time on it. It will stop being as interesting to you. Things we don't know are always much scarier than things that we do, and you will know this one really well. Once you've broken through that irrational fear that comes from not knowing the parameters of what could happen if you lost your job, you will find it easier to accept the following:

- I'm not afraid of losing my job because it will probably never happen.
- If it does happen, it is not under my control.
- Regardless of when it happens, it is not happening now.
- When it does happen, I'll still be me, I'll be fine.

Who Are You?

In earlier pages, there was a focus on fearing things that mostly never happen, the illusion of control, and the importance of now. But the last point mentioned earlier—that you will still be you—hasn't been discussed, and it is probably the most important. It is the hardest to "get" but if you do get it, or mostly get it, you won't have any fears left.

A SAMURAI LEADER STORY

Mary Jo, a pretty 5' 2" brunette straight out of college with a degree in computer science had already lined up a job with a good consulting firm. Then she heard of a job with NASA where she would be building training systems for advanced missile systems for the F-16 program for the US Air Force. She quickly observed that the competition for the job was all male, all aerospace engineers, and all seemingly "the cream of the crop" (as she was repeatedly reminded during the interview process). Just the job description was intimidating!

During the interview, she was asked one critical question. The NASA interviewer laid out the complexity of the work resulting from the difficulty of the technical work, the number of subcontractors involved, the politics of a civilian/military effort, and working in a secure environment. He then asked her how she would go about performing the project. She paused, thought, and replied, "One step at a time."

She got the job. She was the only computer science engineer hired and the only woman. She had to travel for long periods of time to air force bases, there dealing with generals, colonels, and other senior officers, all who

*doubted that this young woman could under-
stand the workings of a complex F-16 flight
simulator, and even more so, its missile systems. Nonetheless, Mary Jo worked though
every issue at every base, confronting them
directly and with no visible hesitation, frequently visiting the subcontractors to ensure
the total reliability of the product. She operated
with precision, always taking one step at a
time. Within a year and a half, she was promoted as a department lead, and all those aerospace engineers ended up working for her.
Projects were always delivered on budget, on
schedule, and successfully implemented.*

As a samurai manager, Mary Jo knew that she
would never know her limits until she tested them—
just as a pilot needs to test the performance characteristics of a new jet fighter before it would be known
what it really could do!

So you need to know, "Who are you?" This is one
of those ultimate questions. We go through life trying
to answer it. It can be answered in any number of ways
at a variety of levels of intellectual depth. A name by
itself doesn't answer it or otherwise everyone named
John Smith would be the same person. At the other
extreme, we could be defined by our fingerprints,

which would guarantee uniqueness, but how would that help (in the absence of a police investigation)?

Most religions offer up partial answers for this question, as do most philosophies. Most people when asked this question offer up neither a religious nor a philosophical answer.

"Hold on. 'Who am I?' What does this have to do with stress and fear?"

EVERYTHING!

Most people answer the question "Who are you?" by referring to something else or something they have, depending on who is asking:

- I am Joey's dad (at a kid's soccer game)
- I am the owner of the new house on the corner (at a neighborhood gathering)
- I am the vice president of XYZ Corporation (at a chamber of commerce meeting)
- I am an eight handicap (at a golf course)
- I am the owner of an original Van Gogh (during cocktails at an art gallery showing)
- I am the owner of a new Porsche 911 Turbo (at every chance possible!)

Given the right opportunity, most people will answer the question by describing what they are proudest of having (in some cases, that means having accomplished, e.g., I was captain of the football team in college or I was CIO of ABC Company). Given enough time, most people will answer the question by describing all the things that they have (or have accomplished). By the time they have finished describing what they have and what they have accomplished, they believe you know who they are. That's because it is the only real definition they have of themselves.

In the business world, the answer for most managers to the question of who they are is their job title. They are the manager of purchasing or the sales director for the southern region. In fact, when introduced to people, they hand over their business card and that tells who they are—and if you don't have a business card, you almost feel like you are part of the anonymous mass of humanity. You barely exist.

The funny thing is, that is not who they are!

The sad thing is, the more they define themselves based on their job title, or what they have (or have accomplished), the more fear can get hold of them.

You Are Not What You Have
Take a moment and answer the question of who you are without referring to anything you have or have accomplished.

"Wait a minute. Why can't I use what I have done or what I have to answer the question?"

Those are only indicators—which may or may not even be particularly valid and at best only represent actions taken in the past. Besides, if everything you think you have is taken away, do you cease to exist? Are you only the sum of all the things you have done? What about all the things you want to do? What about the things you tried to do but failed at? Don't those things matter? Maybe a more important description of who you are would be all the things you want to have—whether you have them or not.

"Is this a trick question?"

Unfortunately, it is not a trick question. "Who am I?" In a universe of unimaginable scope and diversity, we exist on a tiny dust mote of a planet among four billion other human beings with essentially identical DNA and yet we still cry out, "I AM!" We are just not sure what to say after that. And we fear that we have nothing more to add. And out of that fear comes the idea that the more things you have, the more you are! So you start acquiring. The more you have, the more you need to have. And it is never enough. And everything can be taken away. Then you are less than you were before, etc., etc., etc.

If you define yourself by what you have, you will never be fearless!

So how do you know who you are?

- In Christianity, the answer to the "who are you?" question is your soul.
- In Zen, the answer to that question is your True Self.

Those two answers are pretty close to being the same. Coming from very different points of view, both Christianity and Zen acknowledge a unique individual spirit in every human being.

Note that in neither case are you defined by what you have.

Since this book is about samurai and samurai managers, the Zen answer will be used. (You can probably get to the same place using the approaches of religions other than Zen.)

If you asked Zen masters the "Who are you" question, their answers would probably be intellectually elusive, perhaps something like "one true person without rank." But the answers would not relate to having things or wanting things or things that they had done or wanted to do.

If you asked Zen masters what they needed, to the extent they answered at all, their answer might be something like, "to make dinner." If pressed further about what was needed, an old-fashioned Zen master would probably hit you with a stick! (Not out of meanness, but as a learning device.) The simplicity of that answer is the foundation of fearlessness.

"This is cool! You're saying that if I can answer that stupid 'who are you?' question I can be fearless?"

You got it!

"Okay, I'm on this. I've been paying attention. I know I am not my bank account or my house or the car I drive. I'm not the job that I do—no matter how important my job is. I am not my family—no matter how terrific they are. So far, so good, right?"

So far.

"I'm not the quarterback for my high school football team—though ten years ago I did get my picture in the sports section of our local paper! I'm not the big deal I just did—though I'm a hero at work right now, I might add. I'm not... Hold on, I'm getting lost again. I think I know who I'm not—although I'm not sure why that isn't who I am—but I seem to have forgotten who I am."

Time for a little more Zen.

Clinging Is Bad!

Most people know that being clingy in a relationship doesn't usually work out very well. Couples break up all the time when one is clinging to the other. Neither one is happy with the situation—especially the one doing the clinging. But the one doing the clinging can imagine no happiness without the other—their sense of self is caught up into being with the other person. This is not a healthy relationship basis. So why do we all do it?

We cling to the attachments that we use to define who we are. These attachments may be other people, they may be the car we drive or the house we own, they may be the job we have or something we've done in our past. For some it may be a set of ideas learned long ago or a new indoctrination. We hold onto these things with a desperate tenacity, fearful every day that they will be taken from us. We cling to these things because without them we fear we are nothing. As stated earlier, they are the way we answer the question of who we are.

It is not the having of things that is the problem. **It is the having to have!** There are actually very few things in life that we have to have. We need air to breathe, food to eat, shelter from the cold, and companionship. We need to raise our children. That's all we really need—and that's very doable for all of us. Man has been doing that for a million years. Everything beyond that is just something that we want. And it is great when we get them—although we pretty much know that getting them really doesn't change that much. But remember, as you free yourself from the having to have of things, you are freeing yourself from the fears of not getting those things.

And when you free yourself of fear, you make it easier to do all the things you want to do and get all the things you want. That may sound twisted, but it is true!

And frankly, we've known for a thousand years that to succeed one MUST NOT have to have things—one can't cling to ideas, to possessions, to people, to desires or ambitions, to signs of status, or to anything else. Cling to anything and you open the doorway to fear. As fear comes to you, your abilities to succeed start shrinking.

From *The Questions of Suvikrantavikramin* (Prajnaparamita Sutras):

To the extent that there is clinging, to that extent is there bondage.

To the extent that there is clinging, to that extent is there no path—to that extent, all is discomfort and distress.

As long as there is clinging, so long is there vain imagination, projection, and conceptual complication.

As long as there is clinging, there is contention, dissent, and argumentation.

As long as there is clinging, there is ignorance, darkness, and folly.

As long as there is clinging, there are fears and there are horrors.

As long as there is clinging, there is the snare of morbidity and the destructiveness of morbidity.

As long as there is clinging, there is harassment by discomfort and seeking of comfort.

The Bodhisattva (a god-like being) seeing these and all the rest does not cling to anything, to anything at all.[13]

Being Cool

Do you want everyone to think you're "cool"? Cool has been cool for a long time. Though most words describing current cultural "hipness" tend to be faddish and disappear quickly (e.g., groovy, the bomb, the cat's pajamas), the word "cool" has endured as an ultimate compliment for a long, long time. Each new generation has adopted it as its own. And its meaning has remained pretty constant. The same attributes define it. No one who is cool ever clings to anything. Someone who is cool, no matter how involved in an activity, no matter how committed to the purpose, still maintains a certain detachment. The moment matters, but what follows does not. There is no attachment to consequences. What happens, happens. By its nature, cool represents the idea of "nonattachment."

Nonattachment

Buddha's third Noble Truth is that suffering can be eliminated by eliminating desire. Take away desire and fear disappears. The desire that is referred to here is the desire for things one doesn't have. And that means you don't have it right NOW! There is no limit on the amount of desire and enjoyment on anything that you have right NOW. The difference between the two states of desire—that of desiring something that you have NOW and desiring something you *do not* have NOW but want in the future—is the difference between coolness and clinging, fearlessness and dependency, nonattachment and suffering.

What this means is that there is no problem with having things. While you have them, enjoy it. If you have a beautiful house, a new car, a great stock portfolio, enjoy the having of it, but don't need to have it tomorrow. It is not who you are. Your coolness depends on not depending on it to be there always. It's there until it is not there and you are the same either way. If it is not there tomorrow, you haven't lost anything that matters. That is nonattachment!

"Now you've gone too far! The reason I work hard is so that I can get things! I really want a bigger house. I want a new car. I want to send my kids to private school. And I want to join a golf club. Getting those things is what makes doing this job worth it. Otherwise, I'd never work this hard and put up with all the stuff I have to put up with!"

This one is tough. So, pick one of the following three choices.

A) Don't do anything different, stay the way you are, and keep your fears and your stress.
B) Remember the importance of "balance" to samurai. It's okay to want those things, just don't need them. Don't sacrifice yourself to the desire for those things. Work hard to get them, do your best, then let it go if it doesn't happen. *Be cool.*
C) It's not about wanting those things or not wanting them. Simplify your life. Meditate more. Detach yourself from what you want to get as a result of your work. When you are working, work—with full attention and commitment. If you don't like doing it, find a job you do like. When financial success follows, enjoy what you choose to acquire; if financial success does not follow, enjoy no less the not-having of things.

So, which answer did you pick?

If you picked A, stop reading, you are wasting your time.

If you picked B, keep reading, that's the samurai/Samurai Leader response.

If you picked C, consider reading much more serious treatises on Zen than this is.

So, Who Are You?

*"By the way, I picked B, so I'm still with this. If
you asked a samurai the 'Who are you?' question,
what would the response be?"*

As long as the samurai wasn't also a Zen master, the
answer would probably be, "I am samurai."

*"I like that. But isn't that like saying, I'm a lawyer
or a doctor?"*

No, because the samurai is describing his way of
being, not an occupation or something that he has.
His concept of himself is a mirror reflection of the
Code of the Samurai. The rightness of his actions, for
him, will be the measure to which they conform to
the code. His true inner voice will sound like a samurai. That takes him a good way down the path, but
not all the way.

The point of the question is to get to one's True
Self—that consciousness inside each of us that in
brief moments breaks free of all the clutter and debris
of falsely acquired personality (that "I" which glories
in the vivid NOWness of a sunset, loves a particular
type of experience, embraces others with no need for
gain, performs a truly charitable act, attains momen-
tarily the clarity of mindfulness). It's that welling up
in your heart that makes certain moments intensely

personal. That self is who you are. But most of us only get glimpses of that self. Its true voice is that little voice inside us that we hear now and again.

- It's the voice of our conscience when we are doing something we should not be doing
- It's the voice that marvels at a newborn baby or the grandeur of the Rocky Mountains
- It's the voice that reports back to us from deep within ourselves

Listen to that voice; it is your True Self trying to get your attention. **It's who you are!**

"But isn't that as far as we are trying to go in this? If I can answer the 'Who are you?' question by saying, 'I'm a Samurai Leader,' then that should be good enough."

We will have done well.

"But I'm not there yet, am I?"

Nope! Knowing what the right answer is and being the answer are two different things. And there's more to being a Samurai Leader that hasn't been covered yet.

Sword Strokes

FINDING YOUR PERFECT JOB

Success is much easier when you're in the job and/or career that is right for you. Okay, you knew that already. But how do you know what it is and how do you know when you have it? The answer lies in that same "Who are you?" question. To get to the answer, you have to do two things: 1) you have to listen to that little voice inside your head (and not all the big voices around you); and 2) you have to identify all of your talents and capabilities (as they really are and not how you would like them to be).

The big voices come from everywhere: one's parents and friends, current cultural "hotties" (like being an actor or a model or whatever is cool at the moment), childhood fixations, needs for status, and especially one's own ego. Ignore the big voices! Listen to that little voice inside you that tells you what you really love doing or being a part of. (Sometimes it actually matches up with a big voice—but don't count on it—and be a little suspicious of it when it appears to.)

When you are identifying your talents, don't just look at "business-related abilities." List *all* your abilities. If you're a good listener, list that. Think of your personality characteristics as "abilities," e.g., patient, energetic, friendly, good talker, etc. Think about how your mind works, what kind of problems is it good at solving, and where it gets hung up. Think of the kind of people you like being around. Come up with a list of your ten greatest abilities.

The right job—the one you can be most successful at—will be the job/career that matches up with that little voice in your head AND requires almost all of your ten greatest abilities. For that job/career, you have been specially designed. Very few others will be as good at it as you are because it doesn't meet their design characteristics. You can do it better because it is who you are.

It is the combination of your passions and your abilities that make you uniquely qualified!

Before we go on, here is a summary of what we have learned in this chapter.

The Keys to Fearlessness
- Do the right thing
- Training is important
- Maintain your skills
- Maintain your physical fitness
- Think positively
- Confront your fear
- Nonattachment
- No clinging
- Be cool

All these things will work together and be mutually reinforcing. Similarly, surrendering the idea of control and focusing one's attention on NOW will also facilitate the right mindset. The key to actually doing all this is simply understanding and discipline. The understanding that is required is that this will drive away fears because of its holistic approach. It all comes together centered on a way of being that is much more "natural" to each of us. It is about being who we really are. It is about detachment from a host of artificial measurements of self that are truly self-destructive.

At first, the challenge of fearlessness seems very daunting. It requires disciplining both mind and body. That's a lot of discipline! But it doesn't have to be done at once. Start anywhere; take whichever starting point seems to be the easiest. Each step taken will make the next one easier.

QUESTIONS TO CONSIDER ─────

1. At work what are the things you think you have to have? Why?

2. What fears that you carry with you would you most like to put aside? What stops you from doing that?

CHAPTER EIGHT

THE WARRIOR MIND
PART I:
MENTAL DISCIPLINE

The swords of a samurai were prized for their histories in battle, the hardness of their metal, and the sharpness of the blades. Yet, in battles the merits of the sword rarely determined who lived and who died. Nor were the most famous swordsmen known for their great strength. Speed could counter strength, but speed unwisely directed could be fatal, too. The master swordsmen took their advantage in other ways: they observed their opponents' way of holding their swords, observed their footwork, spotted their tendencies, and then devised tactics that would prevail. Their battles were won first in their mind. Then in the swordfight, the master's sword and mind were seamlessly wedded to the purpose, without hesitation or doubt.

Samurai Leaders get no swords to slash opponents. Their minds will have to be enough. Unfortunately, the minds of most managers are not really in fighting shape—they are dull and rusty from too much passive thought, like warriors too long in peacetime. Their minds strain to see through the fogs of preconceptions and prejudgments, insufficient information, and too much data. Most minds were never properly trained to begin with and confuse intellectual power with wisdom. Most minds have so many bad habits that seeing what is in front of them is a challenge often failed and seeing what isn't there is literally inconceivable.

Training the Mind

Samurai Leaders working with mindfulness can see both what is there and what isn't there. But in the same way that the mind had to be reformed before the goal of fearlessness could be achieved, in order to get to mindfulness, the mind once more needs retraining. Moreover, to escape the bonds of passivity, it needs to be channeled and disciplined to aggressively contend with business challenges and opportunities.

In the movie *The Gods Must Be Crazy,* an African bushman finds an empty Coke bottle that had been tossed out by the pilot of a low-flying airplane. Not knowing what it was, he took it back to the members of his tribe and they discovered a number of uses for it, from cooking utensil to weapon. Given how little they had in the form of possessions, it was recognized as having great value. Because they had no preconception of what it was, their minds were not limited as to its uses. Ultimately, though, the Coke bottle caused dissension in the tribe as they fought over who would control this new asset. Recognizing that the burden of dealing with the rights and uses associated with the bottle was too high, they resolved to give it back to the gods from whom they believed it had come.

This movie contains a number of lessons for the Samurai Leader. Foremost is the demonstration of the benefit of approaching an asset without preconceptions. Too often managers fail to see the value of assets under their management because their minds are constrained to seeing those assets traditionally. They "see" based on previous experiences and become locked in to a limited and unimaginative viewpoint. This results in "not being able to see what's right in front of you."

In the same way that training is an important element of fearlessness, so must the mind be trained to get it into fighting shape. The following poem is quoted from an early seventeenth century text on fighting tactics written by Yagyu Munenori, a famed samurai:

It is the mind
that is the mind
confusing the mind.
Do not leave the mind,
O mind,
To the mind.[14]

Many factors restrain the mind from achieving clarity of thought for a Samurai Leader:

- preconceptions
- prejudgments
- emotional filtering
- lack of focus
- attachments
- passivity

There are other factors that could be mentioned, but these particular ones pertain to the samurai/Zen ideals. Note also that none of these factors are driven by or relate to a person's IQ or overall intelligence. Improvement with respect to each of these factors listed is within the control of the individual. Simply put, by altering one's approach to thinking, one can substantially improve one's clarity of thought. Samurai strove to do so; a Samurai Leader can as well.

Mental Clarity

In Zen, in order to achieve full mindfulness—a true clarity of mind—one strives for a mental "emptiness." This term requires a new definition. Emptiness is a state of mind where there are no preconceptions or biases. In this state, a mind doesn't seek definitions of things, it neither construes nor deconstructs; it disdains opinions and views. Its goal is full awareness of reality by avoiding all limitations from subjective perceptions. It is neither nihilistic nor dismissive. It is not about mental blankness or about ignoring what one perceives. It is not even something one can seek; the fact of seeking it, by applying some definitional standard for it, would keep one from it. It resides already within one's True Self.

Simply put, the path to mental clarity requires training the mind to stop deceiving itself:

- to stop the mind from thinking it knows an answer before it actually knows the answer
- to stop confusing opinions with facts
- to stop limiting the reality of things by imposing definitions which are by their nature incomplete
- to stop emotions from setting up the parameters of understanding
- to stop the mind from blocking all that one's senses can perceive
- to stop the mind from assuming that one's senses can perceive all realities

"Wait a minute—you're getting me confused. If I got this right, you're saying I can't trust my senses, I treat opinions as facts, my emotions get in the way of my thinking...and so most of the things I think I know—I don't really know."

Yes, that's about right.

"But if I can't trust my mind, how am I ever supposed to make a decision?"

I didn't say you couldn't trust your mind. Just the opposite, the capability of your mind is incredible. It is much more intelligent than you think it is. It is capable of much better thinking than you allow it.

"Really?"

Yes. Here are some odds and ends of things that may help you get the point.

"I was so angry I couldn't think straight." Anger isn't the only emotion that keeps one from thinking straight. What about greed, lust, fear, or jealousy and envy? Do you think you think straight when those emotions are involved?

When you see a duck on a lake, you know it exists. But when it dives underwater and you can no longer see it (perceive it with your senses), does it cease to exist?

For several thousand years, we treated the opinion that Earth was the center of the universe as a fact. For most of mankind's existence, most of the "major" facts we believed to be true were false. Many great discoveries occurred as a result of seeking something else. Most religions treat every other religion as false. (Subjective truth? I'm right, everyone else is wrong.)

The point is, most people pay far more attention to taking care of their appearance than they do to taking care of their minds. We've learned that the body needs exercise to function best. And to be in fighting shape we can't just feed it a lot of junk food. But who exercises their mind—who takes their mind out for a walk or run? And think of all the crap we put into our minds. We eat so much mental junk food it is a wonder we can think at all!

Moreover, we believe that learning and thinking are the same thing. Ambitious managers want to learn what they need to succeed—they know they don't know everything. And many of them work at learning from books on management techniques and leadership guides. They try to learn from their experiences and they hope to learn from mentors and bosses. In fact, they are constantly and ubiquitously being told what to do.

But rarely, however, is anyone helping them to improve the way they *think*.

Training Techniques

"Okay, I understand what you're saying, but how do I do it?"

This is going to sound very much like what you do to achieve fearlessness. This is not a coincidence. Many of the same characteristics that lead to stress and fears also inhibit clarity of thought and true mindfulness. As with fearlessness, benefits can be achieved by degree. The mind's bad habits can be reduced one at a time. However, greater results will occur with a coordinated and combined approach.

- **Think of doing the right thing**
- **Train the mind**
- **Think aggressively**
- **Think free of attachments**
- **Think objectively**

Again, it should be noted that each of these approaches to thinking are doable by the average manager. Each can be accomplished by degree. There is no practicable end state to them. They are pathways, which if taken all the way, lead to a powerful, intuitive, imaginative mind, free of boundaries. This goal is accessible to everyone; it is not just for some self-defined intellectually gifted set of individuals—which is not to say that everyone will do it. There is competitive advantage to be gained.

Think of Doing the Right Thing
The mind functions best when it is not in conflict with itself. Thinking in terms of right and wrong is natural for all but the pathological. The essential requirement

here is to have a set of values available and trusted to be used as the guideposts for one's thoughts. Samurai had the code. Within a management context, a Samurai Leader requires a code as well, hence the development of a Samurai Leader Code.

One need read no further than the newspaper accounts of events at Enron and WorldCom, and on Wall Street generally during the recent stock boom, to see how warped the thinking can be when right and wrong don't enter into the mental calculation. With criminal and civil charges being brought against so many intelligent people, one has to wonder: what were they thinking? Couldn't they see that their activities would sooner or later come to light and a day of reckoning would occur? At WorldCom, they tried to hide $11 billion! Enron became a vast financial shell game! *What were they thinking?* These are not stories of just a few individuals, although only a few will actually go to jail. There were many, many people who participated in these massive frauds who failed to exercise any critical judgment. In retrospect, they must be asking themselves: why didn't I see that coming? How could I have been so stupid?

In contrast, compare the clarity of thought of the whistleblowers, the ones who did not succumb to the greed. Somehow, with less information available to them, they could see clearly not only what was occurring but what the consequences would be. Shell games can't be maintained. Why could the whistleblowers see it? They were not any smarter. They were not more experienced. But their minds were functioning more clearly. Their thought processes were not in conflict. They were trying to do the right thing.

A SAMURAI LEADER STORY

In the spring of 2000, everyone watched as the market in Internet stocks started to slide. No one liked to use the word "crash" and many persisted in their optimism. "Wait till September," the Chairman of iCAST said. "You'll see. We'll have a bad summer but by September, we'll be off to the races again."

Margaret, the CEO of iCAST (owned by CMGI) wasn't convinced—but neither had she ever much liked panic. Like most of the CEOs around her, she didn't believe in a drastic change of course. But she did start to think hard. If the market did come back, that was fine—but what if it didn't? What should they do? If fortune favors the prepared mind, what could she do to prepare hers?

She looked at the numbers again and again. They ran model after model, scenario after scenario. P2P went from standing for peer-to-peer to path-to-profitability. iCAST's P2P sure looked long. They were a young start-up running a big, cash-hungry business to build an online entertainment site with self-publishing software allowing musicians and filmmakers to put their works online. It was a big idea in a big market with big players. Their path to profitability took about five expensive years. Margaret and her team could find no shorter path.

Margaret had built companies from scratch in the US and UK, some with venture capital funding and some bootstrapped. She liked bootstrapping more than many people because it's so transparent and she was, intrinsically, a rather stingy person. She really liked not spending money. So, she was not averse to cutting spending all the way to the bone. But she knew from experience that bootstrapping was not an option for iCAST. It didn't solve the fundamental problem.

Come September, the market did not rebound. And she knew what would happen next: lots of pressure to cut costs, lots of layoffs, and lots and lots of redrafts of the business plan. She didn't fear the hard work or even the pain. What she believed was that none of it would be worth it. No amount of layoffs or new budgets would get them across the profitability finish line in time. She had two options: sell the business to someone who *could afford it, or close it. When they failed to conclude a sale, she pushed for what she saw as the only alternative: close it down.*

Her peers were shocked. They were moving heaven and earth to restructure and survive; she was pleading for euthanasia. In the corporate world, survival is success—but not every company survives. She didn't want to cling on, reinventing a vision with ever-decreasing hopes of success. She didn't want to fool herself and she really didn't want to fool the people who counted on her. She urged the chairman (the owner representative from CMGI) to close iCAST down.

As they went into contingency planning, she was urged not to tell the staff what was happening. But the company had extremely smart people, many of whom had been in Internet-based companies for years Most were avid stock traders. Everyone could see what was happening.

Choosing to close rather than stagger on meant iCAST could give everyone decent severance packages. Their vendors were treated with respect and paid off. Everyone had PCs, phones, and offices with which to turn the company into a recruiting club. Day after day, employees would come in from interviews saying, "I had no idea how much I'd achieved here until I started talking about it in this interview." Everyone who wanted work found it and many teams stuck together. What could have been a horrible situation turned into a great one, with everyone providing support, encouragement, and respect. Because they didn't have to slam the door in anyone's face, everyone emerged with their professional reputation intact.

The future Margaret had foreseen did come to pass. Many of her peers struggled on and on, only to close when there was no time and no money left. Severance came to seem a luxury and vendors went away empty-handed. Employees joining a tidal wave of unemployed technology workers found it harder and harder to find work and felt abandoned by their company and their colleagues.

It's a funny thing to be proud of closing your company. But the way Margaret looked at it is this: in every business decision you make, there's a good way to do it and a bad way. (If you're lucky, there are many good ones and not so many bad ones—but you can't count on that.) The bad ones are seductive because they make you think you're avoiding conflict. They look like success because they're easier to do and feel more comfortable. They're mostly short term and mostly they're what everyone wants you to do. The good ones challenge your self-esteem, they challenge received wisdom, and sometimes all they do is keep a bad situation from being much worse.

Margaret's decision to shut the company down is one of the toughest decisions a leader can make. It hurts and it's hard! It's an affront to one's vanity and an admission of defeat for the CEO—and costs the CEO his or her job. But history proves that sometimes it's the right decision. Good leaders act on what is best for the company and its employees, even when it is not what is best for them. Frankly, many other CEOs either blinded their minds to what they knew or didn't have the courage to act on it. But what separated Margaret from the others was that she confronted the facts objectively and squarely and determined what was the right thing to do. Then because it was the right thing, she did it.

Train the Mind

Recent studies show that an individual's intelligence level continues to evolve, both positively and negatively, throughout one's lifetime. The brain reacts positively to stimuli and negatively to the lack thereof. Like a muscle, lack of use causes entropy. But there is no need to resort to neurological studies to know that we can train our minds to think more clearly. Most of us are familiar with mnemonic aids to improve memory. We know we think best when we are relaxed and fresh and our attention is focused.

The ability to focus is a matter of mental discipline. Discipline is always a function of training. An undisciplined child may be testing new energies and exploring new territories, but can easily get into trouble and be upsetting to many people around the child; an undisciplined soldier can be a danger to himself and others; an undisciplined mind can result in a lifetime of wasted potential.

What does it mean for a mind to be "undisciplined" and why is it a bad thing?

An undisciplined mind cannot stay focused on a problem to think clearly through to a solution. It gets distracted and loses the threads of logic and insight. It wanders off on tangents. It loses the forest for the trees. Rather than absorbing facts and arguments, it glosses over them, never really understanding the relevancy. It identifies the shallow and the mundane and accepts them as the deep and the true. *It does these things all the time!* Gradually the possessor of an undisciplined mind, and those people who interact with that mind, lose confidence in their mental ability, which causes doubt, which is also debilitating. Faced with these doubts it grows more passive, less willing to think adventurously, aggressively. It becomes a copycat mind, afraid of originality.

This pretty much describes the way most people think. **It doesn't have to be this way!**

Everyone can improve by staying focused longer and focusing deeper. The first step is simple: get rid of the external distractions. When it comes to needing to focus, there is no such thing as multi-processing. No, you can't read the report and listen to jazz in the background. You can't write an analysis and watch the football game or the kids. For those who like the background music because it is relaxing, remember the idea is that your mind should not be comfortable. That just leads to a passive awareness. To function at its best, one's mind needs to be actively committed to awareness. So, begin by removing the external factors that hinder the mind from aggressively focusing.

Of course, the real enemy of the mind's capability to focus is the mind itself. The worst distractions come from within. Overheated and frenetic, a myriad of thoughts cascade through our minds, blocking out the subject of focus. As one tries to digest financial statements, thoughts of personal relationships, sporting events, personnel matters at work, consequences of not doing a good job, what's for dinner, all interfere with concentrating on the financial statements—with the result that one's understanding of what is revealed in the statements is fragmentary and limited and some necessary insight is missed. This is not because of lack of intelligence, but because of lack of focus.

The key is to train the mind to be calm and diligent. This is one of the main purposes of meditation. As discussed earlier, while meditating, the mind is being disciplined to be quiet and stay focused. This really works. You learn that you can control your own mind. For longer and longer periods of time it stays focused where you want it to. And it goes deeper, no longer just skating across the tops of meanings and perceptions. The extraneous thoughts are put aside while the mind seeks out new understandings, makes connections, and finds solutions not previously visible. Ironically, this is what your mind wants to do. And it will do it naturally when it is not distracted. This enhanced concentration transfers directly to the work environment. The more one focuses on things, the easier it is to do.

Start by listening to people at work. Really listen without planning in your mind what you want to say. Try listening so intently that you anticipate what they are about to say, before they say it. (But don't tell them what they are about to say—that's really annoying!) In meetings where your role is not active, try watching everything, hearing everything, without thinking about anything. Like a sponge, just absorb it all without making judgments. Let awareness flow in without biasing thoughts accompanying it. Practice awareness whenever you can—while driving, just drive without any music, without thinking of anything, just observing what is going on with all the cars around you, their relative speeds, the traffic flows, which other drivers don't seem to be paying attention because they've got cell phones to their ears. As you practice this full awareness, you'll get better at it. At work, you'll soon be amazed at all you see and understand.

Think Aggressively

Thinking aggressively is another form of training the mind. Law schools specialize in this. A law student is taught to come up with opposing arguments, to rebut and refute the opinions of others, to not listen passively. Passive thought and action is to be avoided. It is not samurai! The goal is a hungry and searching mind that seeks out the true meanings and connections, that sees the weaknesses and flaws in policies and procedures, opinions and action plans. An active mind strives to find the best answers. It doesn't accept the first idea that comes along; it challenges every idea to test its mettle.

This is easier to do than it sounds. When you think you have come up with an answer to a problem, see how many other answers you can come up with. Then pick the best one. Then force yourself to take an opposing view and argue why it's wrong. Imagine you are the boss; from his perspective, how does your answer look? Never stop with the first thought that occurs to you. That is lazy thinking.

Make sure you are seeing not only what is there, but what isn't there. Most managers have trouble seeing what is in the "white space." The best business deals are found there. How can you get one plus one to equal three (or more)? What risks are out there that haven't manifested themselves yet?

One way to start doing this is to predict the future. Really, it isn't hard. Begin by thinking how your industry will be different in ten years in the future. Some things will be obvious. Focus on the biggest changes. There, you just predicted the future. The real problem isn't predicting what happens in the future, the problem is predicting when it is going to happen and what will be the consequences of its happening. But that isn't so hard when you know what you are looking for. Now the challenge is just to watch for the early indicators of the changes and manage accordingly. The white space now comes into focus.

The key to thinking aggressively is to train your mind to challenge everything.

- Are the "facts" true? Are there new facts that weren't considered previously?
- Are some of the facts actually just opinions?
- Has the "current" thinking actually become dated?
- Is it time to reconsider certain traditional judgment calls?

- Has the competitive environment changed but strategies stayed the same?

The mind needs to be trained to Attack! Attack! Attack!

Sword Strokes

THINKING BACKWARDS

Sometimes it helps to think backwards.

If a manager's goal is only to achieve marginal improvement, traditional "forward-oriented" thinking will probably be adequate. You start with what you have and you try to get a little more of it to keep your boss happy. You take what has worked before and try to do it a little better. But what do you do to get 30 percent year over year growth instead of just 5 percent? To do that consistently you have to change the way you think. You won't usually succeed just by trying to run that much faster or squeeze productivity that much more.

Instead of looking at what you have and thinking about how to maximize it, create a very aggressive goal and think about what has to happen to achieve that. It takes a different way of thinking and a different set of actions to achieve very aggressive goals. Try thinking backwards by starting with the goal having been achieved. What does the operating environment look like that supports that achievement? What drove the achieving of it? What kind of people are then going to be on the team? What were the key success factors that helped make it happen?

What you are likely to discover is that some of the things that you just identified as being part of that great achievement are not currently at hand. You don't have all the resources that are going to be required. You don't have all the right people. You are wasting resources on things that can only produce marginal success. But now you know what you need to do. You have seen the future. Now it is just a function of putting the pieces together that produce the success. (But don't forget to still get the day-to-day stuff done!)

To achieve great success, reverse engineer your dreams!

The next chapter will go much further into how to discipline your mind to make it as sharp as a samurai's sword. The last two training topics, thinking with non-attachment and objectivity, will be presented. But for now, the key take-away is that your mind, like your body, needs care and maintenance. The mind is organic and functions optimally when it is active, challenged, focused, and in a healthy environment. And, strangely enough, it is at its best when it is trying to do what is right.

QUESTIONS TO CONSIDER

1. Is your mind "in good shape" or is it overweight and lazy?

2. Does your mind have a mind of its own?

CHAPTER NINE

THE WARRIOR MIND

PART II:
MENTAL DETACHMENT

Zen Master Shoushan would hold up a stick and say, "If you call this a stick, you are clinging. If you do not call it a stick, you are ignoring. So what do you call it?"

This simple koan contains the key to clarity of mind. To a Zen master, the act of calling it a stick is clinging because of the preconceived definition that accompanies the act of calling it a stick. We are all familiar with the idea of a stick, we have seen them around us all of our lives. With that definition, the nature of the stick becomes artificially limited. Locked in by preconceptions of what a "stick" is, one fails to see its full potentialities. However, if one doesn't call it a stick, one is ignoring the truth of certain perceptions. It is not "not a stick."

The basis for this duality is the Zen awareness that things have both perceptual characteristics and nonperceptual characteristics. Seeing the duck sitting on the lake presents its perceptual characteristics. When it dives under the water, there is no longer a perceptual basis, its existence can't be known in that moment through any of the five senses (seeing, hearing, tasting, smelling, feeling) but one *knows* it still exists.

In order to "know" beyond the perceptual and subjective barriers of thought, one must go beyond names, forms, and definitions. One cannot carry forward preconceptions, opinions, and views. The bushmen who found the Coke bottle had no attachments to a concept or definition of what a Coke bottle was. Accordingly, they approached it with a free and creative mind, unbounded by any preconceptions or limitations on its utility.

"Wait a minute! Why do I care if it's a stick or not? And what good does that Coke bottle do me? Shoot, Cokes don't even come in glass bottles anymore!"

This isn't about Coke bottles or sticks. Seeing without attachments is important because a manager has under his or her control all sorts of assets (people, manufacturing capabilities, equipment, financial resources, etc.), all of which can be used in ways that they have not been used in the past *if that manager can "see" their full potential for uses in the future!*

The next two sections are absolutely fundamental to improving one's ability to think clearly and creatively.

They are the key to seeing into the future. And you'll be surprised at how intuitively obvious it all is.

Thinking without Attachment

It is essential for a manager in business today to think with nonattachment. The pace of change is too rapid, the global competition too transforming, for a manager to hold onto ways of doing things that used to work, to define assets based on how they used to be used or valued, to see opportunities only where they used to be found. If one's thinking is attached to past practices, the bias of the attachment will hinder development and growth.

Yet remember, it is ignoring if one does not call it a stick. The fact that the world is changing does not mean that all past practices are no longer meaningful or useful. An attachment to always going to the new and different, to always seeking the next evolution or revolution of things, is also a destructive limitation. That bias in favor of change will also hinder development and growth.

"Wait a minute! First, it isn't a stick, then it's a stick. I can't be attached to the past, but I can't be not attached to it. You're making me confused!"

You are not confused—but the ideas may be confusing. The problem with this idea of mental nonattachment is that it is another version of the "who are you" dilemma. People feel confused when they don't know what they are supposed to believe. Note the word "feel" used there. It is a feeling of being upset, promoted by the mind.

Our minds hate paradox. In an uncertain world, the mind strives for certainty. Again because of our million years of evolving in an hostile environment, in order to ensure our survival, our minds developed to define and characterize things—helpful or harmful, useful or useless, friend or foe. But with civilization came greater complexity and the mind's tendencies toward classification became a limiting factor, not a survival factor.

Our very sense of self—the "who am I" issue—is trapped in the mental attachments that are formed. People define themselves based on attachments to certain conglomerations of ideas.

- "I am a political conservative."
- "I am a good husband."
- "I am a devout Christian."
- "I am a dumb jock."
- "I am an environmentalist."
- "I am a tough manager."

String these sets of ideas together and *PRESTO!,* a person is defined: "I am Joe, a politically conservative, devout Christian, a good husband, and a tough manager at work." Now we all think we know Joe because we know the ideas he is attached to. More importantly, Joe thinks he knows Joe because he has defined himself with these sets of ideas. The stronger Joe attaches to his adopted sets of ideas, the more rigid and inflexible he becomes. Worse yet, these sets of ideas are usually derived from other people with other agendas—they weren't custom fitted for Joe.

Once these sets of ideas solidify in our minds, we start shutting down other legitimate options and limit ourselves to that narrow way of being that falls within our self-sustaining definitions. But a jock may discover he enjoys opera. A republican may discover he prefers a democratic candidate. Someone who thinks of himself as a tough manager may find that being friendlier and trusting his employees works better. In other words, as one's life experiences accumulate, the ideas one attaches to must evolve. Finally, as one gains true insight into the world as it is, as one attains wisdom, one discovers there is no need to attach to any sets of ideas.

Removing Idea Sets

This lack of attachment to pre-established sets of ideas is particularly important to a Samurai Leader because of the dynamism and diversity of the business environment. Any mind set that locks a manager into a rigid way of looking at the world and determining courses of action is inviting long-term career disaster. The cheese is going to move!

The challenge in discarding one's attachment to these "idea sets" is that one's self-image is itself attached to them. In the prior chapter on fearlessness, consideration was given to answering the "who am I?" question without referring to things one has and things one has done. This next stage of nonattachment requires surrendering our historically developed prepackaged sets of ideas that we use to define ourselves—that constitute a ready-made, intellectually premised, self-image.

Note that the problem here isn't that ideas tend to form into natural sets that are intellectually consistent. The problem is that one can't be attached to any particular set in a way that biases one's thinking and results in prejudgments. All that does is restrict the natural power of one's mind to find the best solutions to new problems.

To the extent our self-image is a reflection of idea sets defining who we think we are, the self-image we carry around with us becomes a barrier to our own growth and development. A self-image based on rigid, pre-established sets of ideas imposes artificial limitations on what one can be. This is easy to understand with respect to individuals with a poor self-image—low self-esteem—but can even be true for those with a "positive" self image.

"Yeah, sure...But that's not me! I'm a confident guy. I was captain of my high school football team. I

went to an Ivy League college. My self-image is fine!
I know who I am."

You probably only know some of who you are, little of who you can be. And most of who you think you are is based on what occurred in the past and in the meantime, you've changed, probably without noticing.

"Not me...I haven't changed. I'm the same guy
I've always been!"

Even if it were true—which it isn't—why would you be proud of that?

"Because it's true—people don't change."

Things Change; People Change

Of course people change—not necessarily for the better. People change because of getting older, changing circumstances, new experiences, learning new things, meeting new people, and a myriad of new influences that occur every year. We change physically, emotionally, and mentally all the time! **But what may not change is our self-image!** And if it doesn't change, it becomes increasingly dated and mired in misconceptions. As that occurs, it becomes harder and harder for people to understand what is going on around them. It becomes harder to think clearly and determine what actions one needs to take.

Let's put this in a business context:

- In a meeting to review his company's marketing strategy, a manager has a new idea about what the company should do. But he doesn't say anything because he doesn't think of himself as someone who has good new ideas. Later in the meeting, someone else comes up with essentially the same idea and everyone loves it.
- A factory level manager, praised for running a tough shop, gets promoted to a staff job. As a "tough manager," he applies what worked for him in the past in his new job. He goes down in flames.

Here is another real life example; you guess what happens:

- A CFO succeeds brilliantly at Company A with a series of cost-cutting actions. He gets hired at Company B, which is also financially troubled.

What's the first thing he is going to do? You already know the answer to this one—in fact, many of you have experienced it personally.

Of course, he ruthlessly cuts costs. That is what worked for him in the past.

Unfortunately, Company B's real problems were on the revenue side. The CFO never saw it because he saw himself as a cost cutter and therefore looked at all financial problems in that context. So, instead of investing time and effort in solving the revenue problem, he cut revenue development resources!

OOPS!

The past never repeats itself identically! If you don't let your self-image evolve and grow, you will fail.

Ideally, any self-image is an unnecessary limitation on who one is. JUST BE. You don't really have to define yourself in order to determine what you should do at any moment of the day. Do the right thing. Open up your mind; free your mind to be its creative, intuitive self.

"You're telling me that even a positive self-image—let alone a negative one—can keep someone from thinking clearly?"

Exactly. Business conditions are constantly changing. What worked yesterday may not work tomorrow. Don't perceive yourself—or let others perceive you—as being locked into a particular set of behaviors. As a manager, one needs to get rid of as many specific self-defining characteristics as possible. Free yourself to be a tough manager when that will work best, and a flexible, sensitive manager in the next assignment; recognize that sometimes it is right to go for the big play and sometimes slow and steady is right. Sometimes you need to trust the people around you and sometimes you shouldn't. Freed of the biases of self-imaging based on specific concepts such as "trusting," "bold," or "tough," your mind will be flexible enough to think clearly about what is **now** as opposed to what was **then**!

A couple of examples might be useful. These examples are infamous and were made at the mega corporation level—so think how many individuals must have failed to see what was coming because they were blinded by their past experience and self-image.

- IBM could have owned and controlled the first versions of the Microsoft operating system. IBM did not see the coming of the personal computer.
- Coca-Cola, the most powerful beverage company in the world, initially missed out on selling high-end bottled water.
- Sears didn't see the threat of the Wal-Mart value proposition.
- General Motors and Ford didn't believe customers would pay for quality. Their business plans were based on planned obsolescence until Toyota and Nissan taught them differently.

These are just a few examples. The list of large corporations who missed what was coming in their own industries and lost huge chunks of business would be a very long list! Companies, even more than individuals, tend to cling to a limited view of what they are and what they do. The more successful they are, the harder it is for them to continue to think clearly about the future. They will cling to what has worked in the past. "Don't fix it if it ain't broke." Their senior execs even know this and still race their herd of buffalo toward the cliff!

Changing Opinions

An attachment to one's self-image is only one of many attachments that create barriers to thinking clearly. Attachments to opinions and perceptions are also limiting. This becomes especially egregious when underlying the opinions and perceptions are biases and prejudices, which is usually the case. In fact, one would be hard-pressed to find opinions that are not built on some form of personal bias or prejudice. Here the reference is not just to the biases such as gender or race, but include the biasing effects of personal experience.

"Hold on... My opinions are very intelligent—and, of course, they are partly based on my experiences. I'd be crazy to ignore the things I've learned from what's happened to me."

Of course, one should learn from personal experience—just don't learn too much. What happened once doesn't necessarily happen again; what happened to one person may not happen to another. Intuitively everyone knows this is true, yet personal experience is a highly biasing factor. Opinions are built on it. That's what makes opinions subjective by their very nature. **They are not facts!** Too many managers are way too attached to what are only subjectively developed opinions.

Do these sound familiar?

- "Everybody cheats on expense accounts."
- "These days companies don't have any loyalty to their employees."
- "Corporations only care about the bottom line."
- "You can't trust employees."
- "Employees don't have any sense of loyalty to their company."

Or how about:

- "You should always go with the new technology."
- "You should never go with the new technology."
- "Take care of your employees first, then your customers, then your shareholders."
- "Take care of the shareholders first, then your customers, then your employees."
- "Take care of your customers first, then your shareholders, then your employees."

The point here is that all the statements above are just opinions, some of which conflict with each other. Nonetheless, many companies manage day to day as if these statements were absolute truths. Yet, any manager knows that the right action to be taken in any particular situation depends on the circumstances. Opinions and perceptions should only be used as guides, not as foundations.

In the practice of Zen, in order to reach true mindfulness, one needs to be unattached to all opinions, unattached to any particular point of view. To fill out any picture of things or events, one must look from a variety of perspectives and maintain a flexible and open awareness.

From *The Questions of Suvikrantavikramin:*

The practice of perfect insight is unexcelled, clear, transcendent. It is inaccessible to any who follow appearances, who follow attainment, who have views of self, who have views of being, who have views of life, who have views of personality, who have views of existence, who have views of non-existence, who have views of nihilism, who have views of permanence, who have views of their own bodies, who have views of the clusters, who have views of the elements, who have views of the sense media, who have views of Buddha...who have views of nirvana,

who have a sense of attainment, or who are con-
ceited, or who act on greed, hatred, or folly, or
who act on unreality, or who are on a wrong
path...the practice of perfect insight is the prac-
tice of rising above all worlds.[15]

To some this may sound like the ultimate
dichotomy: that to be wise one must not know anything. That is not what is being said. Rather, it
preaches that to be wise one must not fixate on any set
of truths or facts; one must not seek final conclusions.
All you need to do is leave your mind free to absorb all
that happens around it and when decisions need to be
made, trust your mind to act appropriately—*it will.*

*"This is hard to understand. This perfect insight
thing is another way of saying being like super
smart—really wise. You sort of know everything, but
you don't have opinions about anything? That
doesn't make any sense!"*

This is just a way to get the clutter out of your
mind. You don't need to refer back to opinions in
order to think about things. Just use awareness—your
mind will do the rest very well by itself when it is not
hemmed in by biases and opinions masquerading as
facts and foundations. You don't have to start with an
opinion in order to determine what course of action to
take. You don't need to have a "view" before you

think about something. That is a form of mental laziness, imposing blinders on your mind. It prevents new and original thought. You will make better decisions if you don't start with opinions and preconceptions. If you start with a "view," it may get in the way of seeing what is there. All sorts of psych tests have shown that people will "see" what they expect to see.

The goal here is to prepare the mind to penetrate into the objective reality of things by exercising awareness (mindfulness). This perfect insight exists inside everyone and, therefore, is not something one has to seek out. It requires no books to be read or sermons to be heard. It does require freeing the mind of all attachments.

Accordingly, the secret to clarity of mind is to be detached from:

- the need to classify and categorize;
- the need to define;
- adherence to a self-image; and
- opinions and preconceptions.

This is not easy to do! It will take conscious effort for a while. And none but the Zen master ever succeeds as a general matter. But with the ever-increasing pace of change in business, no leader will succeed for long holding onto any set of views and opinions.

We are almost done, but there is one more high hurdle to jump!

Think Objectively

Graduate students in philosophy love to debate the issues, such as subjective versus objective reality. What is the meaning of truth? It is a great topic to discuss over beers at the end of a workday. For a Samurai Leader, when it comes to doing business, however, objective reality wins. That means that truth —reality—is found outside ourselves. That means to think objectively one needs to escape the confines of our emotional landscape.

That means when it comes to thinking clearly, emotions are almost always a bad thing!

The mental distortions caused by emotions such as anger, love, and hate are known to all of us. Angry people do stupid things, so do people in love. The mind seems to get trapped in the emotional swamp of those emotions and clarity of thought disappears. Those emotions, when exaggerated, can have extreme effects on one's mental processing. But all emotions can create, to a lesser or greater degree, barriers and warps to clarity and mindfulness.

From the *Avatamsaka Sutra (The Flower Ornament Scripture):*

Ignorant creatures produce sprouts of subsequent mundane life because of continually slipping into erroneous views, because of

*minds shrouded by the darkness of ignorance,
because of being puffed up with pride, because
of conceptions, because of mental fixations of
desires caught in the net of craving, because of
hopes pursued by actions in the tangle of deceit
and falsehood, because of deeds connected
with envy and jealousy producing mundane
states, because of accumulation of actions rife
with greed, hatred, and folly, because of the
flames of mind ignited by anger and resentment, because of undertakings bound up with
delusion, because of seeds in the mind, intel-
lect, and consciousness bound to the flows of
craving, existence, and ignorance.*[16]

Just within this passage, the emotions of pride,
desires and cravings, hope, envy and jealousy, greed,
hatred, anger, and resentment are identified as barriers to clarity of thought and mindfulness. Moreover,
it is clear that actions produced by these emotions
lead to folly and ignorance.

A Samurai Leader needs to note that most of these
negative emotions are common in the workplace. They
influence relationships and decisions every day.
However, they are camouflaged. Sophisticated managers have learned not to let their emotions show. They
try to hide their greed, their envy, their pride, and their
anger. But their cravings for attention and status,
power, and success are imbedded in all their decisions.

A Samurai Leader needs to both subdue his own emotional needs as well as learn how to identify and manipulate the emotional drivers of coworkers, bosses, customers, and suppliers. As one masters one's own emotional flows, it becomes much easier to master the emotional flows of others.

"Hold up! Now I'm supposed to get rid of all my emotions? Even the good ones? Like love and compassion? That wouldn't make me a very good person!"

You make a good point. One's emotions are important. However, to be a Samurai Leader, one cannot let emotions cloud thinking. A certain amount of emotional detachment is essential. At a minimum, emotional balance must be achieved and emotional control must be maintained. Just burying emotions under a calm exterior is not enough. That won't produce the clarity and focus that one's mind needs to think best. Do whatever works best for you, but before important business decisions are reached, make sure you have obtained some emotional equanimity. (Something as simple as taking a brief walk can be settling, but for larger issues, the approaches that promote fearlessness will usually work.)

Also, there is a distinction between trying to do the right thing driven by *emotions* such as love and compassion, and trying to do the right thing based on *values* such as love and compassion. Again, this is a matter of a certain detachment in order to ensure clarity of thought. The distinction is important though because bad decisions can be reached even when driven by the most benevolent of emotions.

Additionally, some emotions are more destructive than others. The intensity of the emotion bears directly on its warping effect on thinking. So once again the samurai approach is recommended: strive to think and act in accordance with the Code. Particular emphasis here would be on maintaining one's mental balance by not succumbing to excessive emotionality.

"So now you're telling me to get rid of the bad emotions, and keep the good ones. But don't let even the good emotions drive my thinking—my values, the Samurai Leader Code, will lead me to making the best decisions. That's asking for an awful lot of control!"

Yes, it is. This isn't easy stuff! But remember, all we are aiming at here is how to make the best business decisions. Decisions in one's personal life are much harder to divorce from emotions (although a Zen master would see no distinction).

When Emotions Enter Anyway
Still, even in business, emotional issues arise that cloud judgment. Things get personal. The more things get

personal, the harder it is to maintain objectivity. As objectivity gets lost, the mind starts focusing on outcomes that are good only for the individual and not the company. Loyalty is lost. As that individual starts thinking (and acting) based on subjective criteria, the optimal business decision may never be discovered.

As emotions and subjectivity take over one's thinking, even simple and apparently good-hearted acts can become confused and even negative. Let's use the issue of corporate charity as an example.

- If a company provides charitable contributions in order to improve it's reputation in the community, that isn't charity. It is public relations.
- If a company promotes charitable events because the senior execs want to feel good about themselves, that's just selfishness at the expense of their shareholders. (Let alone if they do it because they like going to the symphony balls, the art gallery openings, and the many other society events surrounding charities!)
- If a company promotes charitable contributions by its employees through political intimidation (mild or otherwise), the very nature of the charitable act is lost. (This happens a lot more than one would think. It is usually driven by whoever is in charge of the annual charity drive needing to show their competence and commitment. Where's the charity in that?)

- If a company makes charitable contributions in reasonable amounts based on its earnings and does so just "to do the right thing," and is not seeking any other reward, that's the real thing! (And because it is the real thing, that demonstration of its values will have a very positive effect on its corporate culture—so it wins anyway!)

Thinking objectively is a fundamental requirement for anyone following the Samurai Code. Doing the right thing, acting honorably and compassionately, being loyal and self-disciplined, becomes impossible when one's first priority is "What do I get out of this?" In order to make the best business decisions for the company one works for, a Samurai Leader needs to be mindless of the personal outcomes that may flow from the decision—both good and bad. The only outcome that matters is achieving the goals of the company. The more a manager can think self-lessly relative to outcomes, the better that manager's thinking will be. (Keep in mind, too, that ironically this approach always works out best in the long run for that manager!)

An obvious example of camouflaged emotions driving business decisions is the world of mergers and acquisitions. In corporate America, one would be hard-pressed to come up with a better example of senior executives and brilliant consultants, advisors and analysts making more bad decisions as a result of subjective thinking based on greed, egotism, and a hunger for power and status. The records show that most mergers and acquisitions never produce the economic returns promised shareholders. Many times, it is not even close! Yet, the conclusions reached after thousands of man-hours of research and analysis always seem to justify the huge investments of capital and the management and employee layoffs that follow.

The reality of the business world is that it is much less objective than appears on the surface. Too many decisions are undermined by emotionally driven personal outcomes contrary to the best interests of the corporation. That is one of the primary reasons there are so few good managers. Over time, the more a manager thinks subjectively, the more likely failure will catch up to him.

"So what you're saying is that the wisest way to move forward is to act in accordance with the right set of values without attachment to a desired set of outcomes, without excessive emotionality. Otherwise, even 'good deeds' can get lost and may even turn into 'bad deeds.'"

Exactly.

Which brings us back to the question from earlier in this chapter—why do smart people do stupid things? Without question, Ms. Stewart is a very intelligent person. Yet, also obviously she made a series of very bad decisions. Even when given time to reflect, she continued to make bad decisions. Since her problems were not a lack of mental capacity, the thinking that led to the bad decisions must have resulted from the emotional barriers that warped her thought processes. Just a guess, but don't greed, arrogance, and selfishness seem likely?

The point here isn't about Ms. Stewart; she is just an obvious example of how emotions cloud judgments. Most times in business situations, the results are not as spectacularly demonstrated as in Ms. Stewart's case. But she is by no means the only one guilty of faulty reasoning by virtue of emotional imbalance. The amount of greed, arrogance, and selfishness among the managers of businesses is overwhelming! Increasingly it is both unproductive and dangerous at both the corporate and the individual level. Yet, those and other emotions continue to negatively drive important business decisions. It occurs every day in every corporation, with respect to issues both great and small. It is a manageable problem that, for the most part, goes unmanaged.

It probably must be admitted that thinking objectively may not be natural to us. Emotions are natural occurrences for every human being, and we all think while we are "feeling things." So of course, it is a challenge to not think based on those feelings. But the benefits of thinking objectively are huge. That's why samurai worked so hard through meditating, through receiving counsel from others, through a rigid self-discipline that sought internal calm and composure, and through adhering to the Code of the Samurai. As stated often earlier in this, all the elements of the code and the Zen lessons presented here work holistically in support of each other. Thinking objectively will flow from all the other actions discussed in this book.

So, to think clearly with mindfulness:

- **Think of doing the right thing.**
- **Train the mind.**
- **Think aggressively.**
- **Think without attachment.**
- **Think objectively.**

QUESTIONS TO CONSIDER

1. In your business, what is your most strongly held opinion? How long ago did you reach that opinion?

2. Who do you go to for wise advice? What is that person like?

CHAPTER TEN

THE SAMURAI COMPANY

Very successful companies like General Electric, IBM, Hewlett-Packard, Marriott, and Merck developed strong cultures based on certain core values. The specific values that were emphasized at these companies varied one to the other, but within each company, the core values were very clearly understood by everyone. At each of those companies, and there are many others like them, there was an appreciation of how essential that company's values were to its continuing success.

There are also many examples today of companies that were destroyed because of their lack of adherence to the right set of core values. In recent times, billions of dollars of market capitalization have been lost because of companies' failures to do the right thing. Thousands of employees have lost their jobs and in many cases lost retirement benefits upon which they were relying. The accounting firm Arthur

Andersen and its one-time client Enron are well-known tragic examples of what can happen to organizations that lose their moral compass, but they are not alone.

Given the dramatic failures in corporate America arising out of the lack of adherence to core values, it is unnecessary here to belabor the point. Everyone now pretty much knows that companies need value codes. However, understanding the need for values and actually establishing them at the company or organizational unit level are two very different things. Three problems quickly arise.

1. What values should be emphasized?
2. How do the values get driven into the company?
3. How do you know the people understand, respect, and accept the values?

As brutally honest business leaders addresses those questions, they must first ask themselves whether it is even realistic to believe that they can create a values code that will be successfully adopted within their company or organizational unit. To do so takes much more than merely getting the right people together to draft a values statement and then posting it on employee bulletin boards.

Moreover, even when corporations do promote certain values, they tend to be limited to a specific core ideology relevant to their particular business. For example, 3M preaches innovation, Hewlett-Packard emphasizes technical contribution, Marriott promotes friendly service at an excellent value, Nordstrom is centered around customer service, and Wal-Mart strives for value for its customers. What is extremely difficult for even the best-managed and most successful companies to do is to present and maintain a broader set of values to its employees, customers, and suppliers. This becomes an almost insurmountable challenge because of:

- high rates of employee turnover at companies;
- merger and acquisition activity;
- continuing changes to business models;
- weaker bonds between employees and their companies;
- global competition for customers;
- increasing cynicism across the population; and
- cultural ADD, where it is hard to get and hold anyone's attention for long enough to get a message across.

More so now than ever before, most employees do not identify closely with the company they work for and do not believe corporate executives preaching values.

"Well, you certainly have painted a pretty bleak picture there! First you say how important values are to a company and then you say they've got no shot at presenting and maintaining anything except a minor set of values—if they can even do that! But somehow I think you will have a Samurai Leader answer for this, too."

You guessed it!

Company Values

The Samurai Code was a foundational set of values not just for the individual samurai but also for the warrior clans to whom they owed allegiance. The leaders of the clans were also samurai and were expected to instill and uphold the same Bushido spirit for the clan. This mutuality of values produced great homogeneity and trust among the leaders and his clansmen. What constituted appropriate behavior was understood by everyone. Respect and responsibility flowed in both directions—both up and down the clan organization. Clarity about what constituted honorable and admirable actions was shared by all. The Samurai Code set guidelines for everyone.

What worked for samurai clans for five hundred years can work for companies, divisions, or business units of whatever size. A samurai values model for a company or business unit has the following advantages:

- Its core values—honor, courage and a warrior spirit, rectitude, loyalty, compassion, honesty, politeness, and self-control—are understandable, complete, and unimpeachable;
- It's a warrior's code, perfect for promoting aggressive business goals like double-digit market share or revenue growth;
- It's identity enhancing—the image of being samurai is very positive in our culture;
- It's attention grabbing, and its concepts are already broadly known, so it will be more easily communicable than most new value messages.

Importantly, additional business-specific values, such as innovation or customer value or customer service, can be grafted onto the Samurai Leader Code based on the particular goals and objectives of the enterprise.

A SAMURAI COMPANY STORY

In 1991, SystemOne Corporation was in deep trouble. As a provider of computer reservation systems to airlines and travel agencies, it was closely tied to Eastern Airlines and Continental Airlines. The failures at both of those companies had dragged

SystemOne into bankruptcy. Industry analysts predicted that SystemOne could not survive and would soon have to close its doors. In the chapter 11 proceeding it was officially valued at $60 million, but there was no one interested in buying it—it was losing tens of millions of dollars and its customers were heading to its competitors. To realize any value from it, it would have to be sold off in pieces. Vultures were circling.

In late 1991, Bill was named CEO and he reshuffled the management team. They set two primary objectives: 1) rebuild the financial structure of the company, and 2) regain the faith in the company of its customers and employees. The first objective was accomplished through a series of financial transactions, each one a triumph of will and creativity. The second objective was ultimately accomplished thanks to a huge natural disaster named Hurricane Andrew.

Hurricane Andrew blew into southern Florida in 1993 with winds in excess of 180 mph. It particularly devastated the area of south Miami, leaving north Miami mostly untouched. SystemOne's headquarters was on the border between south and north Miami and its operational capabilities survived the storm. However, half of its one thousand Miami-based

*employees and many of its travel agency cus-
tomers lived in south Miami. SystemOne's
executive team knew it had to do something—
but what? From the TV news reports and personal, limited tours, it was clear that the
destruction in south Miami was enormous; it
looked like a war zone where a major artillery
battle had been fought.*

*The executive team reached a simple conclu-
sion: they were going to do everything they
could possibly do to help their employees and
customers. It started with finding out who was
okay and who wasn't. They started a search to
find everyone. They identified the problems
that those people living in south Miami had to
deal with—everything from houses buried
under trees to an inability to get cash or emergency funding. For every problem they identified, they set in motion a solution. Soon the
whole company was involved; everyone
wanted to help their coworkers.*

*The solutions varied. The company issued
emergency loans; all it took was an employee's
signature. A floor at headquarters was turned
into a daycare center and everyone took turns
watching over the kids. Customers who had
lost their offices were set up in the company's
technical center to take care of basic operations.
Food and clothes were gathered and distributed*

to the victims of the hurricane. But probably nothing made a bigger impression than the brigade of pickup trucks loaded with emergency items, ice, and chainsaws arriving at the devastated, roofless, and debris-buried home of a fellow employee or customer. The arrival of these SWAT teams of coworkers there to help do whatever was necessary, when things looked hopeless and when no help was expected, transformed both those getting the assistance and those giving it.

After Hurricane Andrew, the values of SystemOne were clear to everyone. The commitment to the values was sincere and unqualified. The standards were set. The talk was walked. The employees knew absolutely that the company cared for them and they loved the company for that. The customers knew it because that caring and attention was passed on to them. That was the value proposition—the company took care of the employees, the employees took care of the customers, and the customers took care of the shareholders. The bonds grew tighter. Competitors learned that there was no point in chasing after SystemOne's customers or employees because they would not leave SystemOne. It was personal.

It did not suddenly get easier for SystemOne, but the progress was steady. The *will and determination to succeed existed at all levels of the company. Management and employees alike were centered on "doing the right thing." Though their competitors were bigger and stronger, they fought for every deal, every sale. They loved their customers. They were samurai.*

SystemOne was ultimately sold to a global player in 1998 for much, much more money than it had been valued at in 1991.

For a company or business unit to go samurai is a huge commitment. It sets strict standards. Living and working to any values code is a daunting challenge, but most times since employees don't expect a manager or the company to actually practice what is preached, failure to adhere to the code is not really noticed. They probably didn't know what the values were anyway.

The Samurai Code as a values code for a company will be noticed. People will know what it means. They will understand it. It will work if given a chance.

PUTTING IT ALL TOGETHER AND WRAPPING IT UP

Practicing a samurai approach to doing business, whether as an individual, as a business unit, or as a whole company, is a comprehensive commitment to a highly principled set of actions. The Samurai Leader will be constantly challenged to perform in accordance with the Code as every day will present hurdles, obstacles, and opportunities to demonstrate one's honor, rectitude, honesty, courage, compassion, loyalty, politeness, and self-control.

In the foregoing chapters, it has been shown how acting samurai will lead to career success. The Code really works. Each element is mutually supportive and each action taken in accordance with the Code makes the next challenge easier to accomplish. Like most disciplined approaches to self-improvement, the more one does it, the easier it gets. You probably understand this by now. But what hasn't really yet been said is anything about what may well be the greatest benefit of being a Samurai Leader.

The greatest benefit goes beyond the sense of fearlessness, which wipes away the pervasive stress inherent in so many business environments. And that is not undervaluing how much better one feels when one wakes up every morning with no fear of what may occur that day, for it truly is a terrific benefit to know that as a warrior you are ready for any battle and unafraid of any consequences.

The greatest benefit goes beyond the sense of confidence one has in knowing that one's mind sees things clearly and objectively and will creatively approach the work that needs to be done. And that is not undervaluing the ability to approach business challenges with an active, open, and insightful intelligence. What a benefit to know that your mind will work for you free of paralyzing doubts and distractions.

The greatest benefit goes beyond the sum of all these individual parts, beyond knowing you do the right thing, unafraid and mindful of everything. It is the joy that comes from putting it all together.

There is only one question left to be answered.

Are you ready to be a Samurai Leader?

APPENDIX A

A LITTLE HISTORY

In feudal Japan, as in Europe in the Middle Ages, certain families rose up and became an aristocracy controlling large estates through force of arms. These nobles relied on trusted retainers to protect and administer their landholdings. As primogeniture was also practiced in Japan, many of these retainers were younger sons and family members. The word *samurai* is in fact derived from *saburau,* meaning, "to serve as an attendant." The word *bushi* is Sino-Japanese for "armed gentry." As these retainers were the ones really running and defending the estates, they became a management class, initially just below the nobility, but ultimately supplanting the nobility who had become mostly absentee landlords.

This samurai class banded into warrior clans by necessity since there was an absence of a strong central government. Over time, certain of these clans became more powerful than the others and created a military government supposedly in the service of the emperor (who was regarded as being the Son of Heaven) but which was in fact the holder of all real power. The first of these military governments, the *Bakufu,* was formed in 1186 in Kamakura, a town not far from present day Tokyo. After a period of fighting among warring factions, the Kamakura Shogunate (the leader of the military regime was called a shogun) was replaced by the Ashikaga era in 1338.

During this era, central control over the various political factions was even more tenuous than during the Kamakura era and the samurai clans were often at war with each other. During the fifteenth and sixteenth centuries, the civil strife was so extensive that those years became known as the Era of Warring States. This was indeed the time for warriors and it is during this period that the Way of the Samurai dominated the culture of Japan.

By the beginning of the seventeenth century, a new political balance was achieved as a result of the strength and strategy of a few warlords who combined under a new shogun, Ieyasu Tokugawa, to establish the Tokugawa era, centered in the town of Edo, now known as Tokyo. The Tokugawa leaders were more capable than their predecessors and maintained far more political and social control. This regime lasted for over two hundred fifty years, not being supplanted until 1868, when the Western world forced open the doors to Japan.

Importantly, during the Tokugawa era, the role of the samurai—but not the importance—began to change. As opportunities to go warring decreased and the fighting among samurai was outlawed, their warrior code was evolved to remain relevant to samurai—now defined by a rigid class structure, not by function—who were serving as administrators, physicians, and even scholars. The Bushido Code was expanded to provide practical and moral guidance as well as to set personal, social, and professional standards of conduct. It should be noted that women born into a samurai family were also deemed samurai.

APPENDIX B

SWORD STROKES

Chapter One

- When you're doing your best work, it will seem effortless!
- Employees can be ruthless imitators.

Chapter Two

- Few managers survive a reputation for being untrustworthy!
- Competitors, whether internal or external, must be taught that nothing can be taken from a Samurai Leader that will not be hard-fought—not even little things. The aggressive predators will go somewhere else that will not be as difficult.
- Remember Management 101! Get the basics right.

Chapter Three

- Samurai Leaders can't ever let problems get the best of them.
- Remember, you are the only one likely to ruin your career!

Chapter Five

- People at all levels of an organization can be helpful—they will more likely help you if you help them!
- The more power a manager *effectively* gives away, the more power that manager has!
- Once it is time to act, everyone's frame of mind should be centered on NOW!

Chapter Six

- Make friends with the gurus!

Chapter Seven

- Sometimes it's wise to take the bullet for the team!
- It is the combination of your passions and your abilities that make you uniquely qualified.

Chapter Eight

- To achieve great success, reverse engineer your dreams!

NOTES

1. From *Hagakure: The Book of the Samurai* by Yamamoto Tsunetomo. Translated by William Scott Wilson and published by Kodansha International. (Hereinafter, "*Hagakure.*")
2. From *Hagakure*.
3. From *Hagakure*.
4. From *Hagakure*.
5. From *Hagakure*.
6. From *Hagakure*.
7. From *Hagakure*.
8. From *Hagakure*.
9. From *The Book of Five Rings* by Miyamoto Musashi (1643). Translated by Thomas Cleary and published by Shambhala Publications, Inc.
10. From *The Book of Family Traditions on the Art of War* by Yagyu Munenori (1632). Translated by Thomas Cleary and published by Shambhala Publications, Inc. (Hereinafter, "Munenori.")
11. From *Good to Great* by Jim Collins p.30.
12. From *Zen and the Art of Insight*, selected and translated by Thomas Cleary and published by Shambhala Publications, Inc., p. 141. (Hereinafter, "*Insight*")
13. From *Insight*, p. 147.
14. From Munenori.
15. From *Insight*, p. 137.
16. From *Insight*, p. 104.

ABOUT THE
AUTHOR

During his thirty years in business, mostly working in the global travel and transportation industry, Bill Diffenderffer has been an attorney specializing in corporate finance, a CEO for leading travel technology companies, a consultant for IBM, and a writer. He is now CEO of Skybus Airlines, an airline seeking to provide ultra-low prices, based in Columbus, Ohio. As an attorney, he led teams negotiating deals worth hundreds of millions of dollars. As a CEO for over ten years, he led companies that ran worldwide computer reservation systems and that built state-of-the-art travel management technology. As a consultant, he advised senior executives at several of the world's largest air carriers, doing work in the United States, Europe, and Asia.

Throughout his career, Bill has been fascinated by the interaction of leadership and execution, analysis and action, values and performance. As a business leader, he found success flowed best when objectives were built on matching values, each holistically supporting the other. While in China and Japan, he discovered intriguing parallels between the needs of business leaders and the Samurai Way.

Bill lives in Columbus, Ohio, and can be contacted at bdiffenderffer@msn.com.

SPECIAL THANKS

This book owes much to those leaders who have shared their experiences in the Samurai Leader Stories. The author truly appreciates the assistance of Gordon Bethune, Bonnie Reitz, Mike Segler, Tom Oliver, Mary Jo Sabeti, Margaret Heffernan, Walt Breidenbach, and Caren Cook Burbach.

The author also owes a big debt to Jill Marsal of the Sandra Dijkstra Literary Agency, who early on saw the promise of the book and whose constructive support and criticism helped make it better. She also found just the right publisher in Sourcebooks, Inc., and a terrific editor in Peter Lynch.

INDEX